Tracing missing persons

An introduction to agencies, methods and sources in England and Wales

BY THE SAME AUTHOR

The family tree detective

Manchester University Press
1983, reprinted 1984, second edition 1985

COLIN D. ROGERS

Tracing missing persons

*An introduction to agencies,
methods and sources
in England and Wales*

MANCHESTER UNIVERSITY PRESS

Published by Manchester University Press
Oxford Road, Manchester M13 9PL, UK
and Wolfeboro, New Hampshire 03894-2069, USA

British Library cataloguing in publication data
Rogers, Colin, *1936–*
   Tracing missing persons in England and Wales: an introduction to agencies, methods
and sources.
   1. Missing persons – England
   I. Title
   362.8   HV6762.G7

Library of Congress Cataloging in publication data
applied for

ISBN 0–7190–1901–X cased

Typeset by Northern Phototypesetting Co, Bolton
Printed and bound in Great Britain
by Biddles Ltd., Guildford and King's Lynn

Contents

		page
Abbreviations		vii
Acknowledgements		viii
Case study A		ix
A step-by-step guide to using the sources described in this book		xiii

A—Introduction   1

B—Agencies

B1	The police	12
B2	The Salvation Army	30
B3	Private detectives	35
B4	Bank trust companies	39
B5	The media	42

C—Sources

C1	Birth	47
C2	Patient records of general practitioners, dentists and opticians	48
C3	The NHS Central Register and Family Practitioner Committee systems	50
C4	Baptism	58
C5	Adoption	59
C6	Affiliation orders	68
C7	Student records	70
C8	Bank accounts	73
C9	Employers' records	78
C10	Unemployment records	86
C11	Voluntary associations, trade unions and professional registers	88
C12	National Insurance	94
C13	The Inland Revenue	100
C14	Marriage	102
C15	Electoral registers	103
C16	The census	109
C17	Prison and Probation Service records	110
C18	Health visitors' records	112
C19	Child benefit	114
C20	Building society investment records	115
C21	Registers of shareholders	120
C22	Estate agents	121
C23	Building society borrowers' records	123

C24 Local authority rates and rents   125
C25 The public utilities – electricity, gas and water board records   127
C26 The telephone system   129
C27 Television licensing and rental records   131
C28 Premium bonds   133
C29 The Drivers Register   135
C30 The Vehicle Register   136
C31 The Police National Computer   138
C32 The Royal Mail redirection service   142
C33 Hospital records   143
C34 Removal firms   147
C35 Passports   148
C36 Holiday and travel records   150
C37 Hotel records   151
C38 Divorce   153
C39 Emigration   154
C40 Retirement pensions   155
C41 Death   157

Appendix I—Runaway children, agencies, and the law   164
Appendix II—Greater Manchester Police 'E' Division
missing persons reports, 1984   169

Case study B   178
Select Bibliography   179
Some useful addresses   182
Index   185

Abbreviations

ABI	Association of British Investigators
ACPO	Association of Chief Police Officers
BBBS	Bradford & Bingley Building Society
BT	British Telecom
AUEW	Amalgamated Union of Engineering Workers
CRO	Criminal Records Office
DE	Department of Employment
DES	Department of Education and Science
DHA	District Health Authority
DHSS	Department of Health and Social Security
DPR	District Probate Registry
DVLC	Driver and Vehicle Licensing Centre
ERO	Electoral Registration Officer
FPC	Family Practitioner Committee
GMC	General Medical Council
GP	General Practitioner
GRO	General Register Office
IBA	Independent Broadcasting Authority
ILEA	Inner London Education Authority
IPI	Institute of Professional Investigators
IPS	International Passenger Survey
LEA	Local Education Authority
MFH	Missing from home
MOD	Ministry of Defence
MPB	Missing Persons Bureau
MRO	Medical Records Officer
NALGO	National Association of Local Government Officers
NCB	National Coal Board
NCCL	National Council for Civil Liberties
NCH	National Children's Home
NHS	National Health Service
NI	National Insurance
NORCAP	National Organisation for the Reunion of Child and Parent
NUM	National Union of Mineworkers
NUPE	National Union of Public Employees
OPCS	Office of Population Censuses and Surveys
PD	Private detective
PIN	Personal Identification Number
PPR	Principal Probate Registry
QTS	Qualified teacher status
SOGAT	Society of Graphical and Allied Trades
T&GWU	Transport and General Workers Union
TSB	Trustee Savings Bank
UAPT	United Association for the Protection of Trade
UKCC	United Kingdom Central Council
USDAW	Union of Shop, Distributive and Allied Workers

Acknowledgements

Without the co-operation of a large number of individuals and institutions, this book would have been quite impossible to write, for it contains many references to current practices which have never previously appeared in print. Much of the data has been collected during visits to these institutions, and I am very grateful to the following for allowing such visits to take place: DHSS Central Records, Newcastle upon Tyne; NHS Central Register, Southport; the General Register Office; the Family Division of the High Court, Somerset House; the Home Office, Queen Anne's Gate; Missing Persons Bureau, New Scotland Yard; various local government departments; regional headquarters of British Telecom, the Post Office, gas, electricity and water boards, and numerous trade unions; banks and bank trust companies; building society branches; personnel departments of various firms, both private and public; Crown Courts and Magistrates Courts; various schools, both public and private; various hospitals, Family Practitioner Committees and Regional/District Health Authorities; estate agents, travel agents, hotels, television rental companies, funeral directors; the Citizens Advice Bureau; several private detectives; Radio Piccadilly; the BBC; Title Research Ltd; the Salvation Army; the Children's Society; the UK Central Council for Nursing, Midwifery and Health Visiting; CCN Systems Guardian Business Information; the Derbyshire Police headquarters; and the Home Office library. For permission to use the case studies I am again indebted to the BBC.

Many visits have been paid to the Greater Manchester Police, to help not only in the construction of section B1 but also with Appendix II.

I have also received help by correspondence from the Inland Revenue, the Driver and Vehicle Licensing Centre, the Department of Employment, the Passport Department of the Home Office, the Department of Education and Science, the Ministry of Defence, the Lord Chancellor's Department, the Bonds and Stock Office, the Television Licensing Centre, the Companies Registration Office, the National Organisation for the Reunion of Child and Parent, British Airways, British Caledonian, the United Association for the Protection of Trade, the Independent Broadcasting Authority, the Police National Computer Unit of the Home Office, the National Children's Home, the National Youth Bureau, the Reunion Register, and several reference librarians.

Most of the above extended this kindness by looking over, and commenting constructively upon, early drafts of the relevant sections of the book.

In addition, some colleagues and friends have provided critical comment on different parts of the book, and to all the above I am extremely grateful. It should also be said that, despite all this, I remain unnervingly capable of making mistakes, for which I alone should be considered responsible.

Case study A—'Anyone knowing the whereabouts of . . .'

(Based on a programme first broadcast on BBC Radio 4 on 22 February 1985.)

The death of Jean Crawford's daughter at the age of six months in 1965 was the result of Fanconi's syndrome, an inherited genetic defect which endangers one quarter of the children whose parents are carriers. The hospital asked for details of other members of the family, and therein lay the problem. Although she could confirm that there was no evidence of the defect on her mother's side, her parents had split up early in the Second World War when Jean was only one year old, and had divorced in 1953, without meeting. The memory of the marriage was so painful that Jean's mother could not, or would not, remember any details about her father's family, and did not know his present whereabouts.

Given such obstacles, Jean's hunt for her father was short-lived; but more recently the problem surfaced in her thoughts as her other children approached the age at which they in turn were to marry. Her mother's attitude had not softened over the years, so this time Jean sought advice on how to go about her search. We first assembled all the facts we knew about him.

Eric Crawford was known to have attended a college in the Manchester area and obtained a qualification in chemistry and engineering, but he had then become a Church of England clergyman. He had married Jean's mother in Middlesex in 1936, and had a reputation for presenting himself as being of a somewhat higher social status than that to which his background entitled him. Seemingly, not much to go on!

The first thing to do was to augment this meagre data by exploiting what little we already knew. The marriage certificate was bought, and showed him to be the son of George Crawford, a 'master hairdresser'. He was twenty-seven at the time of his marriage, and called himself 'Eric Hugh' Crawford, somewhat to Jean's surprise. *Crockford's Clerical Directory*, which listed Anglican clergy almost annually in those days, was able to fill out more of his career – it gave the name of his technical college, where he received his clerical training, and where he served as a priest. By 1941, he was in a diocese in the South East, having a small parish, and teaching in the cathedral town.

From 1941 until 1950, however, the entry in Crockford's did not change, and then disappeared. There was no obituary in the appropriate volumes, and it seemed as though the editor had received no further information about him since the start of the War – later confirmed by Crockford's in correspondence. He disappeared also from the local directories and electoral register at the same time, but he must have lived on because of the evidence of the later divorce.

The reason for the search should have worked for us, as a good deed in someone's medical favour is relatively easy to elicit. We went to the college where Jean's father had been a student and found the registrar willing to waive his normal rule of confidentiality. The record showed Eric Crawford's home address when he was a student in 1927, and the electoral register for that address showed that George and Angelina Crawford had lived there until the mid-1930s, since before the First World War. In the local directories, George was listed as simply a 'barber'; it looked as though the story that Eric liked to exaggerate his own social position was correct.

'Anyone knowing the whereabouts of the relatives of George and Angelina Crawford. . . .' We tried all channels of the local media – letters to newspapers, and little news items in both newspapers and on local radio – all to no avail. A visit to the address proved even more frustrating – the council estate which had been built on the same site was now in a state of decay!

Perhaps, after all, Eric himself had died since the divorce. A search of the national death indexes at St Catherine's House was kindly undertaken on our behalf by a friend; this was a long job, as in this case both 'Eric' and 'Eric Hugh' had to be checked – but once again, there was no sign of him. Had he emigrated? We wondered whether, even if we could get a letter to him, he would reply anyway; but the standard route, through the National Insurance records, was not available because we could not supply an address since 1946. Nor was the NHS route available, because although we could have elicited the support of Jean's GP for contact to be established, Jean's mother no longer had her original identity number which would have been issued when she lived with Eric in 1939.

Then we had a breakthrough. We contacted the bishop of the diocese where Eric had served in the 1930s, and the school where he had taught. Once our bona fides were established, the mystery of

Eric's disappearance in 1941 was explained – he had been sent to jail in the East Midlands for an offence involving boys at the school, and then lost all contact with his former colleagues despite their efforts to keep in touch. This probably explained the reluctance of Jean's mother to help, and of course led to another impasse.

It seemed that we had exhausted the avenues open to us to find Jean's father, but to complete the record, as it were, we had a look at the final decree of the divorce, obtained through Somerset House in London. To our surprise, this supplied the clue we needed. Eric had changed his name, probably on his release from jail, and now called himself Eric Hugh Manning-Crawford.

Immediately we had to ask the question once again: is he still alive? This time, a result, though not the one Jean had hoped for. There was a death entry for a man of this name in 1973, albeit two years younger than her father – but the certificate left no doubt that it was the same man, as he was described as a former schoolmaster and priest. We contacted the man who had reported the death to the registrar, but he did not remember Eric at all – the man had worked for the local social services department, and had the responsibility for making such reports when there was no-one else to do so. Eric had died a pauper.

Oddly, although this had the imaginable effect on Jean personally, it now worked in her favour. The social services department was able to tell us which funeral director they had used, and in the first of several coincidences in this case, he proved to be one of my own former students. He was able to tell us not only where Jean's father was buried, but also the name and address of the only person to come to the funeral. The former piece of information would not have been available from any official record, even though the burial was as recent as 1973.

From the grave register, we were taken to the exact spot where Eric lay, a 'public' grave – on which Jean was not allowed to erect a stone. It was about ten yards from the railway line along which Jean had travelled for years on her way to and from work. Neighbours, and the distant relative who had come to the funeral, told her the story of how Eric had been looking after his aged mother in 1973, but when he had dispatched her in an ambulance on her last journey before her death, he had collapsed on the garden path and himself died on the way to hospital.

No other relatives were known, and so the purpose of the original quest had been fulfilled – there was no-one to question, and no-one to warn about Fanconi's syndrome. Then, as a BBC programme was being prepared on this story, Jean saw, quite by chance, a newspaper advertisement. 'Anyone knowing the whereabouts of relatives of Angelina Crawford please contact. . . .' Eric's mother had not died after all; she had remained in a geriatric hospital since 1973, and had just died, aged 97.

In some ways, this story had a happy ending. Jean used the money which had accumulated in her grandmother's pension to buy lifting equipment and a netting bed to assist nurses and other patients in the hospital. Had she not identified the lady, this money would have reverted to the State. She was told, however, about the many other elderly patients who have received no visitors for many years – the hospital cannot advertise because of the NHS rules on confidentiality of patient data. Reader, are you sure that no such patients are related to you?

A step-by-step guide to using the sources described in this book

(MP = Missing or lost-contact person)

1   If a person is missing from their usual place of abode, report the fact to the police (B1).

2   If the MP is to be the subject of longtitudinal research, without the need for direct contact, refer to C3 (medical research only) and C12.

3   If you wish to discover the present whereabouts of the MP, go to 3.1 below.

4   If it is sufficient for you to reach the MP by letter, go to 4.1 below.

5   For those in search of natural parents, refer to C5 and C6.

3.1 Can the MP be located in the national probate or death indexes (C41)? If not, go to 3.2.

3.2 Is the name sufficiently distinctive to locate it in telephone books (C26) or electoral registers (C15)? If not, go to 3.3.

3.3 Is the MP known to have been a shareholder (C21)? If not, go to 3.4.

3.4 Is the MP likely to be a member of a trade or professional association, or society, or likely to be found in a town/county directory (C11, C15)? If not, go to 3.5.

3.5 Can a more up-to-date address be obtained via the national indexes of birth (C1) if the MP might have had a child, or those of marriage (C14)? See also records of baptism (C4). If not, go to 3.6.

3.6 Leg work is now required (see the Introduction). Compare the present list of residents with those living there at the time of the MP's disappearance, via directories or, preferably, the electoral registers (C15). Contact those who might help with information about the MP's subsequent movements – friends, relatives, business, and so on. Advertising in the area can also help (B5). If this fails, call in outside assistance – go to 3.7.

3.7 The Salvation Army (B2) will help to locate adult relatives. Private detectives can be hired to locate any MP (B3).

4.1 Obtain an address since 1946, if necessary via the records in

3.1–3.5, and 4.2, and go to C12 (co-ordinating also C19 and C40). If this fails, go to 4.2.

4.2 Obtain more up-to-date addresses from, or have letters forwarded to, one or more of C22–25, C32 or C34. If this fails, go to 4.3.

4.3 Try to make contact through the records of any institution with which the MP was associated, e.g. educational (C7), employers (C9, C10, C13), professional or trade associations or societies (C11), hospitals (C33), prisons (C17) or financial transactions (C8, C20, C28). If this fails, go to 4.4.

4.4 Does the MP have children below the age of 25? Refer to C18. If not, go to 4.5.

4.5 Did the MP rent a television set (C27), have a driving licence (C29) or own a car (C30)? If not, go to 4.6.

4.6 Was the MP met on holiday? Refer to C36 and C37.

4.7 Do you suspect that the MP has emigrated? Refer to C35, C12, C39 and C40.

If the above fail, go to 3.6.

A—Introduction

The 'missing persons' of this book's title are defined widely. Whereas the phrase is often taken to mean 'those reported missing to the police', the purpose of this book is to show how to contact anyone alive in England and Wales, or to discover whether they have emigrated or died. It should be of help, therefore, to those who wish to trace not only an errant spouse or, to a small extent, a teenage runaway, but also former friends, colleagues or acquaintances, long-lost relatives, debtors, natural parents, subjects for medical (or other) research, beneficiaries, witnesses, subjects for media interest, and so on. It may be of value also to anyone having an interest in civil liberties, especially when the Data Protection Act comes into force, and an archival curiosity in how we are recorded by different institutions in society.

There is, therefore, no real boundary to missing persons as defined above, though methods used specifically for the apprehension of persons who are also 'wanted' by the police on suspicion are excluded (on grounds of common sense as well as the author's incompetence). The general public has no access to those mechanisms which can identify individuals beyond doubt, such as retinal patterns and fingerprinting – both digital and genetic.

In one important sense, we are all 'missing persons'. Just as beauty is in the eye of the beholder, rather than being a characteristic of those who believe themselves to be beautiful, persons are 'missing' more in the minds of those who wish to trace them; and only when the police are asked to search do they become statistics in the eyes of the State. Those statistics, examined in Section B1, are extraordinary for a number of reasons. The police produce no national figures because some chief constables do not report (or even know) those relating to their area. Estimates by extrapolation are not straightforward because the proportion of those so reported varies widely, by a factor of over five, from one constabulary to another. Taking this into account, however, my guess is that in England and Wales, an average of some 350 persons are reported missing to the police *every day*. Furthermore, the few bits of evidence from this country and the USA suggest that the number who *actually* go missing from their normal abode, without leaving the means to find them, is probably twice that figure.

Sensing the enormous and unnecessary degree of suffering to those left behind, some MPs have raised the issue in the House of Commons, notably Leslie Huckfield and Greville Janner. In 1973, and again in 1983, Mr Janner tried to probe the reality behind the inadequate statistics about missing persons, and to discover which government departments were prepared to help by forwarding mail on behalf of relatives. The production of national statistics was refused on grounds of the 'disproportionate cost' of working them out; his proposal to set up a central registry of missing persons was rejected as superfluous in view of the Metropolitan Police's Central Index; his request to have a Home Office enquiry into the methods used to trace missing persons was turned down because it was a matter for the police; and his worries concerning the distress caused by missing spouses and children were matched by government satisfaction with the effectiveness of police operations. On 23 May 1985 the Prime Minister repeated this confidence in turning down a request from Peter Bruinvels 'to initiate a nation-wide campaign to assist distressed parents in locating their missing children'.

My interest in writing the book was, in the first instance, genealogical – to enable individuals to learn more about their living relatives, and to facilitate contact between them. Even without a genealogical motive, many people write to newspapers asking for information on the whereabouts of those friends or relations with whom they have lost contact, and it seemed to me quite extraordinary that anyone should have any difficulty in reaching them. Genealogists are, however, used to dealing with the dead, and it comes as something of a shock to the system when living, breathing, and, above all, feeling beings appear at the other end of a documentary labyrinth. Suddenly, I had entered the realms of privacy, civil liberties, public interest versus confidentiality, and Section 2 of the 1911 Official Secrets Act.

Nevertheless, those who trace missing persons often have to adopt the keen eye of the genealogist in finding which documents are available to solve a particular problem, and that more than anything explains the slant which the book takes. It is not *about* missing persons, on whom in this country all too little has been written, and too little research undertaken. Explanations for the changing patterns of teenage runaways or of debt absconders need to be offered by a sociologist, not an archivist. From the USA, a much clearer picture has emerged (see Brennan *et al.*, 1978, the National Youth Work

Alliance, 1979 and *The Times*, 8 January, 1986). There, research into the motivation of *teenage* runaways has shown how easy it is to make premature and misleading judgements based on inadequate statistics, the runaway problem being attributed in the popular Press to any perceived malaise current in society, whether it be the Depression of the thirties, the high rate of marital breakdown, the relative independence of young people, personality disorders, or juvenile delinquency. An added difficulty is the question of *intent* – just because individuals are reported missing, it does not mean necessarily that they have deliberately left home – some are lost, or ill; some are victims of harm, or simply did not realise that their absence from home for a day or two would be the cause of distress. In brief, the American results indicate that there is no single cause for *intentional* running away, but there are common patterns which may be used as predictors in four-fifths of the juvenile cases. Most important is the state of their relationship with their parents; a general feeling of rejection by them, especially if compounded with the threat of punishment, frequent changes of address, alcoholism, or the absence of one parent being the background to most cases. Running away was often an unpremeditated response to a family crisis, but there were also warning signals that such a crisis is approaching: anger; battles over greater autonomy; staying out late at night; and verbal threats of running away, for example.

Further factors which seemed to combine with a less than harmonious home background were the young people's reaction to school and peer group. Most thought themselves to be failures at school, believed that their teachers also thought them failures, and received little educational encouragement from home. Peer group relationships were more complex, but they tended to have fewer peer *group* or community activities; yet they spent more time with their peers, and were more influenced by anti-social pressures.

It is clear that in the UK running away from home is not *in itself* regarded as delinquent activity, though it is often one side-effect; this is particularly highlighted when, evidently beyond parental control, runaways are placed in local authority care. Similarly, a substantial proportion of adults reported missing have left institutions, rather than their own homes. The causes of adults running away from home have received little or no attention from social psychologists, but the motives are obviously very different in those cases which can be identified as intentional.

What interests me more are the activities of the seeker rather than the sought; the methods and motives of different organisations professionally involved in locating missing persons on the public's behalf; and above all the ways in which individuals in our society are documented in 1985, both markedly different from 1885, and in a new world altogether from 1785.

If you wish to locate individuals in England and Wales (to which, broadly speaking, the same systems apply, whereas in many respects Scotland and Ireland differ), the agencies and sources which are available to help you relate to who you are, and the purpose of your enquiry. Broadly speaking, if an individual who would be considered (by the mythical 'reasonable person') as vulnerable is missing from his normal place of abode, then the fact should be reported to the local police. These certainly include anyone under the age of seventeen, the mentally or physically handicapped, the sick, and the aged. However, many normal adults are also reported, and the police must at first treat every case as a potential victim of harm.

While long-term cases remain on police files for investigation, low priority is given (unofficially) to healthy adults who have evidently disappeared of their own free will. Other agencies may then be appropriate for assistance. If the missing person is a close relative over the age of 17, the main agency to which most people turn is the Salvation Army, though if there is financial hardship involved, the local authority's social services department or the DHSS will assist – for example, in maintenance or affiliation cases.

Alternatively, especially where close, adult relatives are not involved, a private detective agency may be brought in. For the appropriate fee, they will take on almost any kind of missing-person case, from adoption to bad debts, and are often able to obtain access to a wide range of records which are unavailable to, or not used by, the Salvation Army.

In an enquiry relating specifically to beneficiaries, your solicitor will probably turn to an agency specialising in such cases; they are also used by bank trust companies when their initial investigations have failed to trace the individuals concerned. A frequent problem for them is the absence of information about the individuals they are seeking: at first, they may not even know of the potential beneficiaries' existence.

Finally, investigative journalists of all the media are notoriously adept at locating people they wish to interview, usually aided by an excellent cuttings indexing system, as well as a willingness to overcome any natural shyness about the invasion of an individual's (or a system's) defences. Section B5 concerns those parts of the media which help enquiries from outsiders, however; journalists have the keen sense of a good story, and an astute enquirer can exploit this in his efforts to gain wide publicity.

Section C sets out a long list of sources which describe, at a specific point or series of points in time, the names and addresses of very large numbers of individuals, most numbering their data subjects in millions. The list does not pretend to be exhaustive – insurance records are omitted, for example, because of the inherent difficulties of knowing whether and where an individual is insured. For each, an attempt is made to answer the following basic questions:

What are the main heads of information contained on the record?
How long is the record kept once the file is no longer 'live'?
What is the significance of any number which the institution allocates to an individual in order to distinguish him from all others?
Who has legitimate access to the data inside the institution?
Who has legitimate access to the data from outside the institution?

The need for the answers to most of these questions is self-evident, except perhaps the third. There is something very personal about a name, almost as if it were part of the individual concerned, and it is one of the first things anyone wishes to know about a new acquaintance. As a means of identification, however, names are very inefficient, and no large organisation can refer to a person by name only. The use of a single name, still prevalent in some parts of the world, died out in this country in the Middle Ages with the acquisition of inherited surnames. The need for two or more forenames was sensed during the population increase at the time of the Industrial Revolution. It is the twentieth century, however, which has seen the widespread practice of distinguishing people by allocating to each a unique number, a practice which lends itself easily to our age of computerisation.

Institutions vary considerably in the systems they use. Some, such as the British Army, have a straightforward numerical allocation, issued chronologically. Others, such as National Insurance, have a slight variation on that same basis. Driving licence and retirement pension numbers have a semi-concealed reference to date of birth. British people have an irrational fear of being given a number, particularly if they feel it is going to be used for more than one purpose. I do not share the fear of being given a National Identity Number because we already have one – the NHS number – which stays with us from birth to death, and is unique to each individual; it is also the number which probably contains the most information coded into it. Yet who complains about it, still less fears it?

From the list of sources in Section C, two categories should be highlighted. The first are those to which the general public have the right of either direct access, or of purchase of data: they are some of the records in C1, 4, 11, 14, 15, 21, 26, 35, 38, and 41. The majority of records in this book, therefore, are not open to public access, and so we must ask how they can be used for tracing missing persons. This, too, will be made evident for each.

Second are some, or all, of the records (as indicated) in C3, 5, 6, 10–13, 16, 17, 19, 26–32, 35, 38, 40 and 41 which are subject to Section 2 of the 1911 Official Secrets Act. While this controversial Section remains on the statute-book, anyone asking to be given data from these records may be not only inviting an official to commit a criminal offence, but also liable to prosecution himself if the disclosure of the information has not been authorised. Section 2 reads as follows:

2.—(1) If any person having in his possession or control any sketch, plan, model, article, note, document, or information which relates to or is used in a prohibited place or anything in such a place, or which has been made or obtained in contravention of this Act, or which has been entrusted in confidence to him by any person holding office under His Majesty or which he has obtained owing to his position as a person who holds or has held office under His Majesty, or as a person who holds or has held a contract made on behalf of his Majesty, or as a person who is or has been employed under a person who holds or has held such an office or contract,—

(a) communicates the sketch, plan, model, article, note, document, or information to any person, other than a person to whom he is authorised to communicate it, or a person to whom it is in the interest of the State his duty to communicate it, or

(b) retains the sketch, plan, model, article, note, or document in his possession or control when he has no right to retain it or when it is contrary to his duty to retain it:

that person shall be guilty of a misdemeanour.

(2) If any person receives any sketch, plan, model, article, note, document, or information, knowing, or having reasonable ground to believe, at the time when he receives it, that the sketch, plan, model, article, note,

document, or information is communicated to him in contravention of this Act he shall be guilty of a misdemeanour, unless he proves that the communication to him of the sketch, plan, model, article, note, document, or information was contrary to his desire.

(3) A person guilty of a misdemeanour under this section shall be liable to imprisonment with or without hard labour for a term not exceeding two years, or to a fine, or to both imprisonment and a fine.

The uses and abuses of this Section are too well-known to need further rehearsal. There have been several campaigns to have it repealed (especially following a prosecution) and replaced by a Freedom of Information Act. In all these debates on its future, however, no serious reformer has advocated the freeing of access to data about private individuals in central government departmental records, though comparisons with overseas practices (concerning, for example, the freedom in Sweden to see other people's tax records) are sometimes made. There can be little doubt that even if Section 2 were to be repealed, such records would be protected either by law or by severe penalties on civil servants who divulged information. Only one official has been prosecuted under this Section for the unauthorised disclosure of commonplace data about ordinary citizens.

However, this apparent Iron Curtain which protects most central government records may be legitimately penetrated in certain circumstances. The key to this apparent contradiction can be found within the written evidence of several departments, including that of the Attorney-General, to the Franks Committee enquiry into the Official Secrets Act. It is the doctrine of self-authorisation, which implies that it is within the competence of ministers and many Civil Servants to give out information, and current practice means that most grades of Civil Servant (save the lowest) are conscious that they can exercise personal judgement on the release of data – the higher the position in the hierarchy, the more that can be released, until a minister *could* release anything from his departmental records, unless it was for personal or political gain. If a senior Civil Servant is satisfied that the release of personal data is in the public interest, or in the interest of the data subject, disclosure would not, in itself, be an offence.

Section B describes the work of the main agencies who engage professionally in tracing missing persons on behalf of members of the public; Section C describes many of the sources which they use, and which may be used by the general public if they go about it in the right way. The simplest technique for making contact is to allow an institution to forward mail to the missing person on your behalf, once you can provide enough information to establish an identification in the appropriate data system. The number of public and private organisations which are willing to do this is so great that it seems difficult to believe that a message cannot be transmitted by one route or another. As will be seen, though, some institutions have an ambivalent attitude towards fowarding mail: to protect the recipient, they might want to know the reason for the request; yet their consciousness of privacy means that they will not ask for the envelope concerned to be left with them unsealed. Many will prefer to overcome this inconsistency by themselves making the approach to the missing person, and telling him of the enquiry.

For some seeking to make contact, the task will be even easier, because most officials, whether public or private, are more willing to help if certain motives are involved. First among these is a medical emergency, particularly where terminal illness or infection is involved; and secondly, the prospect that it is substantially in the financial interest of the missing person to be located. It is important to have proof of the authenticity of such a claim, because institutions have been deceived too many times by charlatans whose real motives for seeking a missing person are somewhat different!

The corollary, by the way, is that there are some motives which, if professed, will normally produce only an adverse reaction. The commonest is probably an attempt to recover a debt, but even worse in its inability to generate a sympathetic response from those in charge of records is romance. Love and bureaucracy do not mix. Each of these motives may be an even stronger, and more genuine, motive than a medical or financial interest, and the negative reaction they invoke has little to do with principle or with reason – it is often because officials fear that, in helping such an enquiry, they may later receive the backlash from a recipient who has been offended by the help given.

There are several reasons why a simple mail-forwarding method of establishing contact might not succeed. The recipient may be dead, or his current address unknown to the data system being used. There are additionally two very common reasons why a forwarded letter might not result in the desired contact: change of name, and unwillingness to respond.

Josling (1985) describes the complications of the law relating to change of name which arise from long custom and practice as much as from statute. The salient issues, from the point of view of this book, are as follows. A person's name is only that by which he is normally known, and there is nothing to prevent him from changing the whole or part of that name unless the purpose is to defraud. Until 1 April 1969, indeed, a child's surname was not even put on the birth entry by the registrar, the surname having to be inferred from that of the parent(s).

No formal certification is required to effect a change of name: usage alone is sufficient. This, however, would lead to considerable difficulties for some organisations – a bank, for example, would find it difficult if a customer claimed to be an account-holder in another name. Such institutions will therefore require some proof that the change has taken place, and may ask for one or more of the following to be produced: a deed poll, notarial instrument, royal licence, Act of Parliament, certificate of confirmation, certificate of marriage, succession to peerage, certificate of adoption, an amended birth certificate, a press advertisement, a certificate of naturalisation, a statutory instrument, a certificate from the court of Lord Lyon of Scotland, a certificate of record in the Book of Council and Session in Scotland, or a certificate of record at the College of Arms. It is this wide variety of methods, and lack of comprehensive indexes, which makes change of name one of the most serious barriers to tracing missing persons.

Of the above, deeds poll are probably the most numerous, and have the advantage of being accessible to the general public if they have been enrolled. Application to see them is at the Filing Department of the Central Office of the Supreme Court (for changes less than three years old) or at the Public Record Office at Chancery Lane, London, for those over three years old. They are enrolled in date order, and the fee at the Central Office is only a few pence. Photocopies of the relevant documents may be purchased. Not all deeds poll *are* enrolled, however, the only advantage being to make it a permanent record.

Even worse than change of name for the seeker of a missing person, is change of identity. Whereas having two identities simultaneously is fairly easy, to change identity completely is much more difficult, and has far-reaching implications for the individual concerned. It has been suggested that writing this book would facilitate such a change; my own view is that, having looked into the consequences, it is much more likely to deter people from doing so. Rejuvenation I could accept; starting a new documentary life would mean losing too much of the old.

If the forwarding of mail fails to produce a response, you will often not know why; but it could be that the recipient does not wish to respond. Any further action will then begin to encroach upon the privacy of the individual. This raises some interesting ethical questions which, I believe, should not be answered in simple generalisations. I would support further action to find anyone who has not responded to requests for help with, for example, medical research into industrial sickness, including those known to have been exposed to radiation from nuclear processes in the Far East or Sellafield; I would certainly seek out witnesses who might help to clear my name from a wrongful prosecution or insurance claim; and I would try to track down anyone who absconded with my payment for goods which I had not received. On the other hand, I would not normally help to find an adopted child, while still a minor, for a natural parent, or to find a battered wife in sanctuary for her husband. (Contact for the latter might be via the National Women's Aid Federation.)

The methods involved, used by all professionals in varying degrees, are basically threefold – the use of publicly available sources; gaining access to data normally closed to the public; and 'leg work', which really means gaining information orally rather than from the written word. Leg work can mean physically visiting relevant addresses in order to question other individuals about a missing person; or it might involve making telephone calls, the preferred method of anyone to whom time is money. For the general public, however, there is little doubt that a successful 'trace' is usually the result of a willingness to use all these methods in combination with each other. To take a simple example, to locate someone whose last-known address is ten years old, a comparison of the two sets of electoral registers will tell you who still lives in the immediate area; a telephone call or a personal visit might reveal the area to which your missing person had moved, the job he had obtained, or other clues as to his present whereabouts. This might then lead to enquiries via a new employer, for example.

Some aspects of leg work are taken further in Section B3, but on the whole it will play a relatively small part in this book, partly because the techniques are simple, few, and fairly obvious, but mainly because my prime interest is in the written record. For in Section C is contained not merely the source material for tracing missing persons, but a description of the way in which we individually, and largely unconsciously, leave behind us a trail of documentary evidence of our existence, from the midwife to the undertaker, which explains the sequence of material in that Section; it also tries to discover how long it lasts, and who has access to it – and therefore to us. Those records which are on computer will from 1987, be open to the individual data subject to inspect and correct if necessary, unless they are exempt under the Data Protection Act. Such exemptions, however, are fairly extensive, especially in the fields of national security, administration of justice, detection of crime, collection of taxes, and data relating to health and social work (see Savage and Edwards, 1984). In this context, data protection is something of a misnomer. Section B3 tries to indicate that, far from adding to the security with which personal data is currently protected, the legislation may have made it more vulnerable to unauthorised disclosure, once the Data Protection Act allows individuals to have access to data held about themselves on computers (from 11 November, 1987).

B—Agencies

B1—The Police

Missing persons, in the colloquial use of the phrase, are normally first reported to the local police, and a section of each force's regulations describes the procedures to be followed whenever a report, usually telephoned, is received. Though issued separately by each force, these procedures are broadly similar to each other – in some parts, indeed, the same word for word. They contain a preliminary categorisation of the cases concerned. While all reports are processed, irrespective of detail, the nature and extent of the action taken will depend largely on whether they are in the category of 'vulnerable'.

Vulnerability is automatically accorded to anyone reported missing who is under eighteen years of age (though in practice, many forces concentrate on the under-seventeens); adults who are over sixty-five, or who are epileptic, diabetic, amnesiac, or suicidal; certain classes of mental patient; and in general anyone to whom, it is reasonably suspected, harm may have befallen.

If persons are missing from their normal place of abode, foul play may be suspected, and it is sometimes difficult to distinguish at first between a person missing for quite innocent reasons, and one who has been murdered and their body hidden. However, there is in practice, though not in theory, a difference in police attitude and procedure between a fifteen-year-old absconding from care for the tenth time, and an eight-year-old who has never been away from supervision before; or between an adult known to be having an affair, and an adult recipient of recent bad news. Ideally, each should be sought as expeditiously as possible, but the numbers of such reports are so great that some priorities must be accorded. The vulnerable are, in the words of one chief constable, given 'much greater attention'.

There is no national index of all missing persons, and I doubt whether such a development would be worth the cost – not because of the importance of the subject, but because such a large number will already have been found before they could be entered. There are no reliable statistics collated nationally; nor does there seem to be any attempt to analyse the causes and categories involved. Sixteen police forces do not maintain a record of the number of cases reported in their area, or are not willing to make them public. Even in England, it does seem surprising that many annual reports of chief constables record the number of stray dogs, but not the number of missing persons; this gives an unfortunate, and of course erroneous, impression of priorities.

The survey which follows draws on figures from eighteen forces which have made them available annually since 1974 (before which local government reorganisation puts an effective barrier on using earlier figures for comparison). A further eight have produced figures for some of those eleven years. Of these twenty-six, many give only overall numbers, so that no analysis of even age or sex is possible in their case. In order to examine a large group of missing persons in more detail than has been available hitherto in this country, the Chief Constable of Greater Manchester has allowed me to study the records of all persons reported missing from one division within the city of Manchester for the year 1984, 1,071 in all, and the results of that analysis appear as Appendix II.

These differences between police forces are, of course, one small aspect of the principle of the relative independence from national control and organisation, and in 1975, the Association of Chief Police Officers decided that the issue of investigating and recording missing persons was one which should remain a matter for individual, rather than national, policy. The result of this devolution, however welcome politically, means that there are major differences in reporting, and in responding to requests for information (cf. *New Society*, 29 July 1982). I am therefore doubly grateful to those forces which were able to respond to my request for figures which had not been published, while understanding that, especially from some data-processing systems, others would have found the extraction of data too costly.

The differences do not end there. The Metropolitan Police routes reports through to the Missing Persons Bureau (MPB) at New Scotland Yard, but although the MPB receives a teleprinter message within minutes of a report being received at a police station, there is a deliberate delay of 48 hours before the actual report forms begin to come through. By that time, some eighty per cent of missing persons have already been found, and the cases are not 'fully recorded' by the MPB. The result, from a statistical point of view, is that figures 'for London' are often very misleading, for they may include any combination of: reports received at any London station, reports 'fully recorded' by the MPB (about one-fifth of the total), and cases referred to the MPB by other forces who suspect that some of their missing cases might have gone to London, including some from abroad.

A further complication is that some forces include absconders from care among their missing persons statistics; others separate them out from the MFH's (Missing From Homes). Unless otherwise stated, I have tried to include absconders in the tables which follow. Whatever system has been developed, each force seems loathe to change what has become their routine way to process their statistics.

Table 1 covers the eleven years for which figures are constantly available, and gives the total number of missing-person reports from the eighteen forces which had published them or supplied them on request. The eighteen include approximately fifty five per cent of the population of England and Wales. The figures in brackets are therefore an extrapolation in order to give some notion of the likely national totals; this extrapolation assumes that the London figure comprises those as reported to Parliament, not only those fully recorded by the MPB.

TABLE 1—*Total number of missing persons reports received by 18 police forces, 1974–84*

1974	56,668	(103,000) (to nearest 500)
1975	62,709	(114,000)
1976	60,008	(109,000)
1977	63,603	(115,500)
1978	61,853	(112,500)
1979	63,667	(116,000)
1980	69,686	(126,500)
1981	76,358	(139,000)
1982	71,049	(129,000)
1983	68,216	(124,000)
1984	66,201	(120,500)

SOURCES Avon and Somerset, Bedfordshire, Cambridgeshire, Cleveland, Derbyshire, Greater Manchester, Hampshire, Hertfordshire, Humberside, Kent, Lancashire, London (MPB only), Nottinghamshire, West Mercia (MFHs only), West Midlands, West Yorkshire, Dyfed-Powys, and North Wales.

The first immediate impression from these figures is the sheer size of the problem. Greater Manchester, London, the West Midlands and West Yorkshire, for example, are each receiving an average of over twenty seven reports of missing persons *daily*. The numbers of these reports have varied over time in a pattern which is broadly similar for most areas – almost random fluctuations during the 1970s followed by a significant increase centering on 1981, followed by a recent and unmistakeable fall. Other areas for which some statistics are available (Cheshire, Leicestershire, Norfolk, South Yorkshire, Suffolk, Sussex and South Wales) also show a decline since 1981. Cleveland and North Wales, however, have exhibited a fairly steady decline in numbers since 1974, falling by about sixty per cent in ten years. Neither the police nor the social services departments in those areas have been able to offer any suggestions as to the cause; there has been no change in the way missing persons are recorded in either area during that period. Since 1981 numbers in Cleveland have increased.

It is easy to jump to simple conclusions in order to explain why, in most areas, there was such a distinct rise and fall in numbers peaking in 1981. When it is seen in Table 3 that the greater part of those reported missing in most if not all areas are juveniles, the rise might be accounted for simply as a reflection of the increased number passing through the fourteen to seventeen age group during those years. However, the actual number of juveniles rose only minutely compared with the rise in the number of missing persons reports, and, in any case, the number of adults also shows the same rise and fall.

Another simple explanation – that changes relate to unemployment – also seems to be disproved by the figures. Unemployment has continued to rise since 1981, and the proportion of missing persons in the population seems to bear little relationship to the proportion of persons registered as unemployed (see Table 2). Areas such as Cleveland, Humberside and South Yorkshire have high rates of unemployment, but moderate or low rates of persons reported missing; West Yorkshire has a moderate rate of unemployment, but a high rate of persons reported missing. Are children more likely to run away from homes in which a parent is unemployed? Does unemployment increase the chances of an erstwhile breadwinner *being* reported missing? Does there come a point when unemployment is so high that it acts as a deterrent to those wishing to break their ties and start a new life? If the recession is having an adverse effect on young people's independence (see *The Guardian*, 24 August 1984), how can we explain the rise in the numbers of young missing persons from 1978 to 1981? Again, only access to large numbers of individual cases would enable even tentative hypotheses to be tested, and it is most unlikely that the police records themselves would include the necessary data. There has certainly been a marked reduction in the proportion of juveniles to all missing persons since 1980 (see Table 4). It will also be

TABLE 2—*Number of persons reported missing and % registered unemployed in same area, 1983*

Area	Persons reported missing	Persons reported missing (per 10,000)	Registered unemployed at 8 December (%)[b]
Avon and Somerset	2,072	15·1	10·5
Bedfordshire	2,008	39·1	10·3
Cambridgeshire	1,601	26·6	10·2
Cheshire	2,318	24·8	13·6
Cleveland	1,280	22·7	20·2
Derbyshire	3,174	34·8	11·3
Gtr. Manchester	11,933	45·9	14·3
Hampshire	3,633	22·4	10·0
Hertfordshire	2,147	22·0	7·4
Humberside	2,414	28·3	15·6
Kent	1,835	12·3	12·0
Lancashire	3,187	23·1	13·6
Leicestershire	2,293	26·5	10·3
London	5,284[a]	7·8(31·1)	9·8
Norfolk	525	7·4	12·1
Nottinghamshire	2,724	27·5	11·6
South Yorkshire	3,951	30·1	15·5
Suffolk	1,110	18·1	9·4
Sussex	3,545	26·2	9·0
West Mercia	2,935	35·3	14·2
West Midlands	11,040	41·5	15·8
West Yorkshire	10,001	48·6	12·4
Wiltshire	1,012	19·0	9·7
Dyfed-Powys	340	7·6	14·6
North Wales	608	9·6	17·4
South Wales	3,875	29·9	15·2

NOTES
(*a*) Fully recorded in the MPB. The figure in brackets allows for the parliamentary estimate of the total number of missing persons reports in London during 1983 (25,000).
(*b*) Source: *Employment Gazette*, January 1984.

noted from Table 2 that the incidence of missing persons reports is by no means even across the country. Some areas have to deal with over six times the problem per head of population than others. In the case of 'E' Division of Greater Manchester, the subject of Appendix II, this figure is twelve times higher than some other counties. Proximity to London has little bearing on the rate; the biggest influence seems to be the degree of urbanisation within each area. Those forces which break down their figures into divisional areas exhibit the same feature – more people are reported missing from the urban areas of a county than from the rural.

When a report first comes into a police station, common sense and experience will determine what initial advice to give, between the extremes of urgent action, and a suggestion to ring back in, say, twelve hours, if the individual is still missing. Sooner or later, however, an essential bureaucracy takes over, with a questionnaire for the informant to fill in. While this may seem to a worried parent to be wasting valuable searching time, the questionnaire is designed to save time later by accumulating all the relevant information in one place. The police will require a physical description (features and health), previous history of running away, addresses of friends and relatives (and school if appropriate), possible reason for disappearance, domestic background, known aliases, occupation, and of course a photograph. A record of clothing is very important because, for the first couple of days at least, it will not normally be changed.

At various intervals thereafter, a number of institutions will be contacted in order to facilitate contact with the missing person. Sometimes this will be automatic, and official – a visit to school to interview a juvenile's friends, for example, or to places of employment. In addition, less public approaches may be made to those institutions which have a policy of confidentiality towards clients and their affairs, and in many cases, the explanation that a certain individual is 'merely' the subject of a missing persons enquiry will elicit a helpful response from, say, a building society or bank manager, a local social security office, or a doctor's receptionist. Without this help given on humanitarian grounds the work of the police in tracing missing adults in particular would be significantly magnified, but the medical profession is restrained by conflicting pressures of confidentiality.

All police officers, whether uniformed or CID, will have some experience of investigating reports of missing persons. Only a few areas appear to have specialist units to deal with the problem, though most forces have a Juvenile Bureau which takes a special interest in the problems of youngsters. The Missing Persons Bureau (MPB) run by the Metropolitan Police acts as a recording and co-ordinating agency, and is not involved directly in the work of tracing. It receives reports from other forces, and from abroad, when it is suspected that the individuals concerned may have come to London. The microcomputer can record a very wide range of distinguishing characteristics, which can subsequently be matched to establish identities. For this reason details of unidentified persons and corpses from all over the country are sent to the MPB, which can then co-ordinate comparisons of dental charts, identification marks used by hospitals and other similar organisations, and details of missing persons which have already been recorded. Even so, it seems surprising that not all long-term missing persons are entered on the MPB's files, and that the MPB is not always informed of the deaths of individuals who have not been identified. Nor, because of confidentiality of patient data, do hospitals always inform the police that they are caring for someone whose identity cannot be established, even when the police ask the question directly.

In 1984 the MPB was asked to look out for 445 missing persons by provincial forces, adding to the 942 still on file from previous years. This figure is somewhat misleading, as the cases counted are only those in which another force forwards a report form – the total number of enquiries by telephone checks or teleprinter messages is considerably above this. However, the number is still dwarfed by those reported from London itself, let alone from the rest of the country. Most of those who do run to London are from the Home Counties, the numbers decreasing with distance, though with a significantly high number from Glasgow and Belfast.

Relatively few persons reported missing are known to the MPB, which is not, therefore, a good source for national statistics on the subject. The great majority, however, will have been entered on the Police National Computer (PNC) almost as soon as the report is received, and a national 'WM number' issued (see p. 140). The number does not distinguish between 'Wanted' and 'Missing', and the entry is wiped from the computer as soon as the person has been located and, in the case of juveniles, returned to a place of safety. Some of the long-term missing will also be entered (at the request of the investigating inspector but on the decision of the editor) in the *Police Gazette*, which has the great advantage over the PNC of being able to carry a much more detailed description, and often a photograph.

All the communications involving the PNC, MPB and *Police Gazette* so far will be confined to the police themselves. However, a decision will be made sooner or later whether to advertise the case more publicly. Occasionally a poster may be issued, though this is rare. The MPB issues about half a dozen a year. The investigating inspector, in conjunction with the force's press office, may arrange for an article to be placed in a newspaper, particularly in local papers which are much more willing to co-operate. Even so, such an article will still be a rarity; of the 1,071 cases analysed in Appendix II, only one was the subject of a press release. The reasons for this apparent reluctance to elicit the help of the general public are probably fivefold. The number of cases for which a newspaper article might be appropriate is so great that neither the papers nor the public would find much interest in them. There is also the difficulty, sometimes, in knowing in which district to advertise, though most will go no further than their own home town. There is also a desire to shield relatives from unwelcome publicity, and a realistic caution because they do not have editorial control over what appears in print. Most important of all, I suspect, is the unwillingness of the police to place examples of missing people constantly in the forefront of the public's consciousness, because that might have the effect of stimulating even more to do the same. During the relatively short-lived campaign by some newspapers in 1985, which ran columns on missing juveniles, there were some successes, but at least one had returned before publication.

If individuals are missing for more than a short time (the length depending on the age, the known habits and last known whereabouts of the individual concerned), other agencies may be asked to assist in a search – mountain rescue, air-sea rescue, rambling clubs, the Armed Forces, friends and neighbours, as well as the police's various specialist teams, such as those of dogs or divers. However, the police will remain in overall control during such an operation. In 1984 a missing adult was discovered dead by a seventeen-year-old schoolgirl, drafted in as part of the Duke of Edinburgh's community service scheme to help short-staffed Kent police. (For a curious view of such searches, see *Police Review*, 10 August 1979.)

Much more controversial is the use of clairvoyants, dowsers, or clairaudients. It is clearly in the interest of those who are professionally involved in these activities to give the impression that the police call upon their help in the more difficult cases, and there is no doubt (from well-documented cases, and from information supplied privately and in confidence by police officers), that they have been uncannily successful in some cases; nor is it to be expected that any professionals would be likely to acknowledge help from amateurs.

I have not found, however, that the police have enough confidence to seek their help (as opposed to accepting their offers of help when all other methods seem to be failing) (see, for example, Cracknell, 1981; the author was involved in the search for Genette Tate). Nor has it been possible to find an official police statement concerning their relationship with clairvoyants. There is a suspicion that they are more successful if there has been foul play; but normal missing-persons cases are far too numerous to interest reporters, and it is only when the length of the investigation means that foul play is more likely that it gets into the Press, and hence to the ears of clairvoyants.

Once *any* missing person is located, the police will probably wish to interview them, a procedure which may understandably be a source of surprise and perhaps annoyance to many parents. The officer will try to determine the cause of the absence and, perhaps more important, the whereabouts while missing. This procedure is designed not only to help if the person is ever reported missing again, but may also be used as a source of criminal intelligence. The needs of missing persons, referred to below, often lure them into the orbit of the criminal fraternity – indeed, some are located almost by accident because they are in the company of characters in whom the police have more than a passing interest, or are questioned in insalubrious neighbourhoods, or late at night, for reasons at first unconnected with the missing-person enquiry. Evidence of criminal activity by those whose cases are analysed in Appendix II does not appear to be great, but the Chief Constable of Bedfordshire observed in his 1982 annual report that, of the missing juveniles found, 'a considerable number became involved in crime during their period of absence'. In the USA, Brennan *et al* (1978) found that of all juvenile runaways, thirty three per cent had been guilty of theft, twenty per cent of selling drugs, twenty eight per cent had used hard drugs, and ten per cent had been involved in break-ins. Shortage of money also drives youngsters in the UK into prostitution.

Juveniles

In several areas, figures are available which distinguish children from adults. Normally, the break-point is the seventeenth birthday, though some forces, such as West Mercia, separate those over eighteen. Table 3 shows the totals and percentages over the eleven years 1974–1984 inclusive in the ten areas where this calculation is possible, showing beyond question that juveniles form the greater part of the problem for the police.

There is some hint in these figures that the more rural areas have the lower proportion of juveniles being reported missing, a difference which applies throughout the eleven-year period; the high figure for

TABLE 3—*Proportion of juveniles reported missing, 1974–84 (by area)*

Area	(i) Total MP reports re juveniles	(ii) Total MP reports	(i) as % of (ii)	% of 10–15s in pop. (1981 census)
Avon and Somerset	12,338	20,835	59·2	9·4
Bedfordshire[a]	9,928	13,747	72·2	10·1
Cleveland	12,898	19,517	66·1	10·6
Derbyshire	27,382	38,544	71·0	9·7
Hertfordshire[b]	14,295	21,910	65·2	9·7
Lancashire	29,335	40,937	71·7	9·6
London	35,182	47,070	74·7	8·4
West Mercia	16,922	23,895	70·8	10·0
Dyfed-Powys	2,025	3,435	58·9	9·1
North Wales	6,373	11,617	54·9	9·8

NOTES (a) Excluding 1982 and 1983.
       (b) Excluding 1974.

TABLE 4—*Proportion of juveniles reported missing, 1974–84 (by year) (from areas listed in Table 3)*

Year	(a) Total MP reports re juveniles	(b) Total MP reports	(a) as % of (b)
1974	16,385	22,713	72·1
1975	15,016	21,347	70·3
1976	14,323	20,782	68·9
1977	13,942	19,757	70·6
1978	15,639	22,340	70·0
1979	15,317	21,460	71·3
1980	16,253	22,999	70·6
1981	16,257	23,823	68·2
1982	15,699	22,686	69·2
1983	13,792	21,027	65·6
1984	14,055	21,531	65·3

London, however, may once again be a reflection of the way in which statistics are recorded, rather than a true indication of a genuinely large juvenile problem. Whereas Table 1 indicated a national trend in terms of absolute numbers being reported, Table 4 shows that there is a remarkable consistency in the proportion of juveniles missing between 1974 and 1984.

A breakdown of the age groups of those reported missing under the age of seventeen is available only for Derbyshire and London, and these are presented separately in Table 5 not only because of the skewing effect of London numbers, but because the age groups are

TABLE 5—*Under-17s reported missing, 1974–84 (Derbyshire and London only)*

	Derbyshire				London			
	u. 14		14–17		u. 14		14–17	
Year	M	F	M	F	M	F	M	F
1974	837	271	1,049	960	321	237	798	1,513
1975	432	289	756	902	330	337	798	1,524
1976	475	245	715	716	317	292	788	1,560
1977	445	215	788	978	353	363	807	1,730
1978	506	205	793	1,259	288	263	903	1,749
1979	400	215	893	965	330	203	899	1,668
1980	315	258	1,010	908	315	258	1,097	1,794
1981	463	161	1,063	799	288	264	881	1,398
1982	467	141	1,132	1,030	393	280	1,390	1,846
1983	424	103	983	790	373	239	1,252	1,594
1984	394[a]		1,604[a]		491	465	925	1,268
1985 (prov.)	—	—	—	—	422	447	861	1,252

NOTE   (a) Sex differences not available.

different in each case, Derbyshire breaking down into under-thirteens and thirteen to sixteen-year-olds, the Metropolitan figures being for under fourteens and fourteen to seventeen-year-olds.

Once again, it should be remembered that the figures for London are those in which the missing person was not located within the first forty-eight hours. Girls are evidently less adventurous than boys in the younger age group. Data from a few other areas which supply the sex of missing juveniles without subdividing the age group suggest that Derbyshire is the more typical of the country as a whole in terms of the male/female differential, though the presence of local authority homes or assessment centres will alter the proportion of teenagers to all missing persons, and the relative numbers of boys and girls, in any one police division.

It should be stressed that all the figures in Tables 1–5 relate to the number of missing persons *reports*, not to the number of missing persons, whose true figure is unknown. A possible indication is given in Appendix II, in which the average *person* had two reports in the same year. It is also clear from that evidence that teenagers are more likely to run away in pairs, or even in groups, if they are in care, whereas most running away from home ran alone.

Appendix II indicates how common it is for the same person to be reported missing more than once in the same year, one fourteen-year-old vanishing seventeen times during 1984, and a seventy-eight year-old twenty-two times. The MPB has records of one child, who between 1973 and 1980, ran away seventy-five times, using eleven different names. One West Country officer, interviewed early in 1984, suggested with tongue in cheek that only a ball and chain would stop one particular eight-year-old from trying to run away to Scotland, where he had been born.

It would be understandable if the policeman on the beat were to show a somewhat ambivalent attitude towards missing minors. According to police policy, all receive priority attention, and all must be considered vulnerable; some, indeed, will have been victims rather than perpetrators of crime, and a few will be found dead, especially in coastal and mountainous areas. Police and public alike will remember for a long time to come the Moors Murders of Brady and Hindley in the early 1960s, whose child victims had been reported missing over a long period. On the other hand, the police are practised enough to know that almost all missing children turn up again, that some will be regarded as a nuisance and not even welcomed back by their parents (some of whom had only reluctantly reported them missing in the first place), and are a considerable drain on police resources.

Investigation of missing-persons reports is indeed a time-consuming exercise. The only detailed estimates of the total man-hours spent in this work comes from the Chief Constable of Hertfordshire who, in a series of reports covering 1974–8, 1981–2 and 1984, indicates that 67,433 hours were spent in looking for 17,915 people. If extrapolated nationally, this suggests that the police in England and Wales provide the full-time equivalent of some 280 officers. Looking for missing juveniles is such a common activity that there is a real danger of casualness by the officers concerned even in methodical mass searches, leading one writer in *Police Review* to suggest rewards in kind for successful teams.

There is a well developed routine laid down in force procedures by which the police investigate reports of missing juveniles. Many, especially the younger ones, are not really missing at all and a thorough search of the home itself will often reveal the children, who have been found in boots of cars, under (or even in) beds, lofts, discarded refrigerators, water-storage tanks, and so on. One small child had been inadvertently washed and put to bed by a next-door neighbour, who had a very large family. Some, however, are found in quite dangerous situations, such as the two and a half year old in

North Wales who was stuck overnight in mud, too deep to move, half a mile from home. The danger can be moral as well as physical – parents are afraid nowadays of a drift into drugs as well as prostitution, and as the latter is taking an increasing number of boys, it is possible that some forces who give more attention to missing girls for that reason should amend their procedures.

If unsuccessful, the search is extended from the home through known relatives and friends, this 'leg work' ensuring that sooner (or not much later) most of these youngsters will turn up. Although there are no hard and fast rules, it seems probable that if teenagers are found living safely with adult relatives or even friends, the police sometimes call upon the social services department to assist in normalising the situation (See Appendix I). Some parents do not even bother to let the police know if a child is found by other means, which can result in more unnecessary leg work, and a possible inflation of the 'still missing' figures.

If a child has been taken by one parent in dispute with another, or is missing from home and under the age of eighteen, the DHSS will help the police to find the individual through the child benefit or National Insurance systems, under authority of circulars issued by both the DHSS and the Home Office. (This help would not be forthcoming, however, if only the spouse had been reported missing.)

In this search for missing minors, the police are rarely helped by the sort of documentary evidence which is available for tracing adults. Juveniles do not enter the public or private bureaucratic systems independently of their parents. One of the few exceptions is the building society investment account which may be held independently by a person of any age who acts responsibly enough to obtain parental approval; bank accounts may be held, but cheque cards virtually impossible to negotiate. Teenage runaways can obtain medical care, including hospital treatment, without providing their NHS numbers. The police are therefore largely dependent on 'leg work' (as defined in the Introduction), and their degree of success in locating youngsters is all the more remarkable.

The reason why so few leave their own area is fairly obvious. Everyone needs food, shelter, money and clothing, the first two most urgently. Warmth and clean clothes are soon missed. These necessities are most easily obtained, in emergency, from relatives and friends who, on the whole, live within easy travelling distance of home (see Brandon et al., 1980 and Wiggans, 1982). The picture of teenagers flocking in large numbers to London is a myth, maintained to a large extent by reporters and dramatists. London, of course, holds out a beckoning hand for most people at some stages of their lives – one eleven-year-old from Bury in 1981 was found walking along a railway line because he thought all lines led to London. In practice, relatively few actually make the journey; of the 3,174 reported missing in Derbyshire in 1983, for example, only three are known to the police to have gone to London, though of course the descriptions of many more are circulated if it is suspected that they are making for the Capital.

Many cities now have organisations which help the homeless, among whom are many who have been reported as missing from home. Such organisations are usually voluntary, though run with some local authority support (see Appendix I). 'Runaway' or 'safe' houses were designed for those really old enough to leave home, but an increasing number in the younger group are using such crisis temporary shelters such as Centre Point in London. In the USA, however, Brennan *et al* (1978) found that the runaway house was relatively little used, except by those who were out for a 'joy ride' experience. Advice to runaways from these voluntary organisations will include reference to the telephone system arranged by the Mothers' Union, by which a runaway can leave a recorded message which will be forwarded home in order to reduce parental worry. I understand, however, that this telephone facility has been very rarely used by the missing teenagers concerned.

Adults

Adults sound in mind and body are given the lowest search priority of all missing persons. English and Houghton (1983) indeed say that no action is normally taken in such cases, and the Citizens Advice Bureau advises anyone seeking assistance that the police do not search for non-vulnerable adults. If, however, they are reported and located, the police response is then to assure the informant (usually the spouse) of the safety of the person concerned, but of their unwillingness to return or to have their whereabouts divulged. It is at this point that the Salvation Army or a private detective agency may be asked to help, for the former will attempt a reconciliation, and the latter will divulge the information which the police would not give. None of the missing spouses in Appendix II traced by the police returned home as a result of being traced. In that very small group, a high number were common-law wives or husbands.

Table 6 shows the rather surprising breakdown of figures relating to missing men and women, adding those available for Cleveland, Dyfed-Powys, Derbyshire, Hertfordshire, Leicestershire and London. Although in any one area, one sex might significantly out-number the other, the statistics indicate that, when spread over time, they are reported missing in roughly equal numbers.

TABLE 6—Over-17s reported missing, 1974–84 (6 areas)

Year	Male	Female
1974	1,386	1,601
1975	1,928	1,606
1976	1,938	1,864
1977	1,366	1,440
1978	1,825	1,937
1979	1,914	1,927
1980	1,982	2,107
1981	2,429	2,200
1982	2,856	2,430
1983	2,496	2,369
1984[a]	2,007	1,858
Total	22,127	21,339

NOTE   (a) Excluding Derbyshire.

In seeking missing adults, the police face problems of the invasion of personal privacy which are not applicable when they are seeking juveniles. They also face the danger of becoming embroiled in the very domestic squabbles which make many adults leave home. The police are now denied access to data from central records of the DHSS at Newcastle, unless the adult is accompanied by a child; yet that branch could help without betraying the missing person's whereabouts (see pp. 98–9). I suspect that they have simply never been asked to do so. A search warrant would not be issued for a straightforward missing-person case, so in theory many of the sources, both public and private, listed in Section C are closed to them. Going missing is not in itself an offence; but every case should be treated as a potential victim of accident or assault, and adequate descriptive files maintained with which unidentified persons or corpses may be compared. Much of the work of tracing missing adults would be saved, given, as the Chief Constable of Derbyshire observed in his report for 1977 (echoing similar pleas made by the Metropolitan Commissioner for over fifty years) that 'often a postcard or telephone call by a Missing Person could have saved many hours of such enquiries'. Sometimes, however, the adults do not even know that they have been reported missing.

The long-term missing

One of the most difficult questions to answer, yet one of the most important, is how many persons reported missing never reappear. Ellison (1964) suggested that of 9,000 who disappear in Britain annually (a gross underestimation even then), some fifty five to sixty per cent never turn up, an estimate with which I cannot agree. There are undoubtedly difficulties in making such an assessment, some of which are beyond the control of the police, and others resulting from the way in which their statistics are presented. Additionally, many people – perhaps even most – do not inform the police in the first place, especially for the fifteen to eighteen age group. In the notorious Nilsen case (the Muswell Hill Murders), only two of the thirteen or so victims had been reported missing, and one of these came from Canada.

If, however, an assessment is made on the basis of the figures available, the first source of data must be the numbers described in the annual reports of many chief constables as 'untraced at 31 December' – five in Cleveland at the end of 1984, for example. Before any conclusions are drawn from these figures, it should be observed that their basis can vary from area to area – and sometimes from year to year within the same area – in a way which is not made explicit in those reports. The phrase can mean 'of all those reported missing during 1983, how many were untraced at the end of the year?'; but it can also mean, 'of all those *ever* reported missing in this area, how many were untraced at the end of the year?'. Nor is it clear in the latter interpretation whether a sixteen year-old, missing for over a year, is still counted in the 'under seventeens still missing' a year later. (This adjustment *is* made by the MPB.) Figures for London are further bedevilled by sometimes including those reported by other forces, so that these may be double-counted in any national total. The MPB does check at regular intervals with all other forces which have asked it to record missing persons from outside the Metropolitan area, in order to make sure that individuals who have returned are no longer on their files.

The difference between these two interpretations is very significant for judging the scale of the *long-term* missing, for many of those who are included as 'still missing at the end of the year' will have been reported for only a short time, and may well turn up within days of the new year. Even using this definition, however, the numbers are relatively small, reflecting the efficiency with which the police conduct their searches (as well as the difficulties faced by those who leave home, and which drive many of them back of their own accord). Taking eight provincial forces for which overall figures are available since 1974 (Cambridgeshire, Derbyshire, Greater Manchester, Hampshire, Kent, Nottinghamshire, West Yorkshire, and North Wales), Table 7 indicates a slight improvement in the rate of success, even when the numbers were increasing.

TABLE 7—Success rate in finding missing persons, 1974–84 (8 provincial police forces)

Year	(a) Missing persons reports	(b) Still missing at 31 December	(b) as % of (a)
1974	31,370	380	1.21
1975	35,561	332	0.93
1976	32,972	304	0.92
1977	33,713	333	0.99
1978	34,451	343	1·00
1979	34,211	285	0·83
1980	37,657	430	1·14
1981	42,277	341	0·80
1982	37,254	311	0·83
1983	35,509	275	0·77
1984	34,527	344	1·00
Total	389,502	3,678	0·94

Of much more significance are figures relating to the length of time between reports of missing persons and their eventual location. In London, sixty-four per cent of girls and seventy-two per cent of boys are found, or returned, within one week; in the USA, Brennan et al. (1978) found that seventy-five per cent of juveniles are located within one week. No similar analysis is available for other forces, except that now to be found in Appendix II.

Occasionally there are references in chief constables' reports to those remaining untraced for more than twelve months. The figures are small, though they vary considerably from area to area: thirty seven untraced in Norfolk at the end of 1983 since 1966; only three untraced in Wiltshire (pre-1984); thirteen missing in West Mercia, but sixty-three in Sussex and twenty-eight in North Wales (all 1982 reports); and three in Suffolk from before 1983. (See also Appendix II.) It may be that figures for the long-term missing are significantly higher in areas where water, especially the sea, prevents the detection of corpses resulting from accident, assault or suicide.

The police can claim much of the credit for this success. Most forces do not prepare statistics on how many missing persons return of their own accord, and how many are traced, though during research for this book I received several rough and ready estimates of 50:50. The Hampshire police report that, of the 47,243 lost and found between 1974 and 1984 inclusive, some forty-three per cent were found by the police while fifty-seven per cent returned voluntarily. In the analysis in Appendix II, the police traced only about one fifth of those reported missing during 1984, the remainder returning of their own accord. The 'majority' in Norfolk returned voluntarily in 1983.

As regards the long-term missing, the reports of the Commissioner for the Metropolitan Police put London once again in a class of its own. Figures supplied in 1985 indicate the number of persons still missing from before 1984 (see Table 8).

TABLE 8—Number of persons still missing (pre-1984)

Area	Female			Male			
	u. 14	14–17	18+	u. 14	14–17	18+	Total
Metropolitan	56	155	260	126	156	347	1,100
Other, and recorded in the MPB	22	78	227	28	77	510	942

NOTE   Only 87 cases prior to 1981 remain unresolved.

The figures in Table 8 seem high, though it is believed that over two-thirds of those under fourteen were actually in the custody of one parent, and reported missing by the other, and that some fifteen per cent had absconded from a local authority home and returned to parents who were itinerant, and therefore not easily traced (*Hansard*, 31 March 1983). Hence one officer could describe to me the position of one missing child as, 'We know where he is – we just can't find him.'

The overall conclusion to be drawn from this survey concerns statistics rather than methodology. Greville Janner's 1973 estimate that 'approximately 150,000 people are going adrift in a year and that approximately 75 per cent of these people are under the age of 18'

(*Hansard*, 14 June 1973) was not too wide of the mark, especially when some measure is given to those who are not reported to the police in the first place. However, the figures for those who return or are traced is also very high, and unless due regard is given to the spectrum of statistics available, especially outside London, the public can be easily misled into believing that the 'legion of the lost' (as one newspaper headline put it) is a massive, endemic problem. Running away *is* endemic; but so is returning, except for the few for whose loved ones left behind there should be considerable sympathy and, in my view, a greater degree of access to the massive data systems described in Section C than is currently the case.

The police can be credited with a great deal of success in tracing missing persons, particularly those who are determined to stay away from home, and are thus left with a comparatively small residue of unsolved cases. However, the gross under-, or overestimates to be found in many articles (for example, *Police Review*, 27 March 1983: the *Sunday Times*, 10 March 1985) are the result of misinterpretation because of the quite inadequate provision of national statistics.

B2—The Salvation Army

Statistics relating to the involvement of the Salvation Army in the work of tracing missing persons are astonishing, reflecting the expertise which has been developed since the foundation of Mrs Bramwell Booth's Enquiry Bureau in 1885, and the unique standing which the organisation holds in this field. Five thousand cases are undertaken annually in Great Britain alone (twenty thousand world-wide), yet only eight full-time case workers with twenty support staff are involved. They, of course, are able to call on the resources of the 25,000 Salvation Army officers in eighty-six countries – few other agents are used.

The operation is regarded as voluntary social work – it receives no government grant, and runs at a financial loss, the fee of £5 covering scarcely one-sixth of the actual costs. Robertson (1965) rightly calls it an 'important adjunct to the welfare state', and it is clear from the research undertaken for this book, particularly Section C, that the Salvation Army is highly regarded by officials as well as the general public. (One said that she would do all she could to help the Salvation Army as she regarded it as a 'responsible public body'; yet in the same interview, she said she was not prepared to help the police!)

The organisation helps not only individuals directly, but also institutions such as local authority social services departments, the NHS, prisons, welfare and probation officers, and responds to requests for help from the police in cases of genuine hardship, medical emergency, and unidentified persons. Clients must be aged seventeen or over.

The success of the Salvation Army in this work rests not only on its own expertise, and the regard in which it is held by the public: its impetus is a commitment to the sanctity of family life, its protection the skill in avoiding bad publicity which follows if even one or two cases came to light in which the Army was misused for a client's ulterior motives. A few words on both aspects may be appropriate here.

The sense of mission does not lead the Salvation Army into cases which are unsuited to its expertise, or those which have a high risk of incurring an emotionally adverse reaction. In particular, they do not undertake a search for anyone under the age of seventeen, or for parents or children separated by adoption or illegitimacy (though siblings so separated might be helped). Nor, because the volume of work is already so large, will they undertake to locate friends, fiancé(e)s or distant relatives. Again, the rather impersonal research involved in genealogy or the distribution of estates is also refused; and, perhaps most significantly, the Salvation Army will not help with the furtherance of divorce proceedings. Richard Williams (1969), who described some of the work of an Army research officer in tracing missing persons, was keen to point out the rather sad fact that for every £1 which it gives towards marriage guidance, the State provides £70 to facilitate divorce. Even without that disparity, however, assistance in these cases would not be forthcoming.

There is, of course, a difficulty in taking this stance. Suppose a spouse, really intending to seek divorce, feigned reconciliation as the objective. The way in which the Salvation Army defends itself against this potential abuse contributes to the second reason for its high standing in the community – the absence of adverse publicity. Indeed, recurrent press stories of the success of many investigations help to maintain their good public image, and the confidence necessary to encourage people to approach them.

This defence is in two parts. The first consists of an application form which requires far more knowledge of the missing person than could be provided by a casual acquaintance or private detective, for example, including physical features, occupational details, and some of the main keys which would allow many of the data systems described in Section C to be accessed. Applicants may be interviewed, preferably alone. The second, and more important in this context, is the policy clearly stated on the application form that addresses will not be divulged without consent. In other words, even if the Salvation Army is deceived as to the purposes of a particular enquiry, the located person will be approached in order to see if they are willing to be contacted by the enquirer. Thus the Army is rarely faced with an irate victim of unwanted attentions, and all the adverse publicity which that would bring. It also, as we shall see, sets the Salvation Army apart from other private enquiry agents who, with a few exceptions, consider themselves the servants of their clients without an obligation to take the interests of the missing person to heart.

Another feature which distinguishes the two agencies is cost, the standard Salvation Army fee being a mere £5 as opposed to private detectives who will operate on a much higher *hourly* rate. They are prepared to waive even this £5 fee in cases of genuine hardship, and for married women seeking their husbands. A loss is probably incurred even in the most simple cases where only forwarding mail is involved, when account is taken of staff time and overheads.

The possibility of State aid for the Investigation Department has been raised in the House of Commons in order to facilitate the work rather than to give the Salvation Army more official standing in government departments. This has not been requested by the Army itself, and I suspect that they might rather retain their independence of action and judgment for as long as they can continue to be independently funded.

In a substantial number of cases, however, perhaps up to fifty per cent, a simple solution such as a letter via Special Section 'A' of the DHSS in Newcastle (see p. 97) does not result in contact; this is especially true in the case of missing women. Months, and even years of more specialised research may be needed, often involving Salvation Army officers normally employed in the remainder of the organisation's operations. Such work, funded by voluntary donations by the public and those who are being helped, eventually brings the success rate to about seventy per cent. This success in finding missing persons occasionally leads to a failure to reunite the family, because some persons located do not wish for a reconciliation, and their wishes are always respected. However, if desired, the Department will act as a 'post-box' redirecting letters, thus keeping a vital link and sometimes building a bridge of reconciliation in so doing.

Williams (1969) illustrated some of the wide variety of cases undertaken by the Salvation Army including a few which, because of their nature, would no longer be accepted. All applicants have to be close relatives of the missing person; but sometimes the development of the skills involved in solving some of the more difficult cases make it hard to resist a challenge. His book also makes it clear that most government agencies offer the Salvation Army few privileges but on the whole are more willing to help within the limits allowed than if an individual or other enquiry agency had been involved.

In 1965, Professor O. R. McGregor of Bedford College, London, was allowed to analyse the Salvation Army's cases. Almost half the enquiries from women were for reconciliation with their husbands, a quarter were for assistance with maintenance payments, and some were simply to discover whether they were still a wife, or a widow. As was to be expected, the most difficult persons to find were those who had changed their name, and those who could easily find casual work, thus breaking a chain of normal employment which allows the Salvation Army to reach an individual through National Insurance or employers' records.

The Army's operation is highly centralised. This reflects the general structure of the organisation, and also guarantees a quality control which would be impossible to maintain if each centre offered the service. It provides for a concentration of expertise, and a channel for international enquiries. Applicants are directed to the headquarters of the Army's Social Services Investigation Department at 110 Middlesex Street, London E1 7HZ (close to Liverpool Street station), though application forms are available from all Salvation Army centres. Please enclose a stamped, addressed envelope – all too few appear to extend this courtesy.

Action taken initially will depend on the amount of information provided, and the circumstances of the individual case. As Richard Williams points out, it is usually easier to trace someone who has been missing for twenty years than twenty days; and most people in immediate distress go to the police anyway. Letters are sent for forwarding through the appropriate public or private agencies, asking those missing to contact the Salvation Army, who will then explain the circumstance of the enquiry. For close relatives, the application form is fairly easy to complete, though a number of applicants do not know the colour of their spouse's eyes or hair, date and place of birth, or even place of occupation!

If these initial letters produce no response, more ingenuity is called for, with approaches made through some of the more unusual sources, a careful sifting of the evidence available, advertising in newspapers, and time-consuming 'leg work', with which private detectives are more associated. In this, the assistance of the national network of Salvation Army officers at over one thousand centres is invaluable. Some of those missing will have gone abroad (see p. 154) and here again the fact that the Salvation Army operates in eighty-six different countries provides a real chance for renewal of contacts which would otherwise be exceedingly improbable.

The officers concerned also act as counsellors, not only for those who come to them in distress, but also to those whom they locate. People do not leave home for no reason, and often that reason is traumatic, whether it be emotional, financial, criminal, or for reasons of health. (If criminals are located, they will be persuaded to give themselves up to the police.) Sometimes the reconciliation of separated spouses is more difficult than the actual location, and painful memories are slow to disappear. The officers are wise enough, once reconciliation has been achieved, to know when it is expedient to withdraw from the case, and they do not automatically keep in touch because of the danger of reopening old wounds. Continued guidance and counselling is available on request, however, whether reconciliation has been effected or not.

One of their many famous cases was that of Noel who, on having to produce his birth certificate in 1975 for an insurance claim, had it pointed out to his astonishment that he had been born a twin, the time of birth being entered in the date column. In this case, the information concerning the missing person was minimal – no name, no sex, and the only evidence for being alive was that the person was forty-one years old. A photograph of the twins, brought together by the Salvation Army, adorns the desk of Lt.-Col. Bramwell Pratt, the Investigation Secretary. Noel's twin had been fostered as a baby. When you read this book, I wonder if you can work out how the case might have been solved?

B3—Private Detectives

Estimates from several sources suggest that about half of the private detectives (PDs) in this country were former policemen who have either retired or left the Force early. Others have come into the profession from a wide variety of occupations, only some of which (such as debt collection or credit agency work) are closely related. Some have followed a correspondence course in order to learn the business. Anyone can establish themselves as a PD, there being no requirement for licensing or membership of a professional body.

It is widely believed that having been in the police must be a distinct advantage in at least three respects – they will bring from police training and experience a knowledge of the way many systems and institutions (especially legal) operate, including the jungle of documentary sources to be found in Section C; they will have a series of friends and contacts who may continue to prove useful; and they will have developed certain skills which will stand them in good stead in their new career – skills of interviewing, for example, or perhaps in the use of electronic devices.

This apparent advantage is not illusory, but it can be easily exaggerated, for the sort of skills which make a first-class PD are not necessarily taught at all – or need not be taught, simply because the police have right of access to certain data banks which are only open to the private sector by stealth. A good PD, many believe, is born, not made.

There are two other divisions within the ranks of the PDs. Some are members of one or more associations which cater for their interests and needs, especially the Association of British Investigators based in Kingston upon Thames. PDs advertise their services in the Yellow Pages (listed under 'Detective Agencies') but do not always incorporate into the advertisement the fact of membership of such an association. The advantages of belonging to such a body are seen to lie mainly in mutual help and advice. The ABI is open to anyone over twenty one who has worked with a detective agency for at least two years, and either passed the Association's examination, 'and/or have otherwise satisfied the Council of their ability, character and integrity'. The other main body, the Institute of Professional Investigators based in Preston, has a much wider membership, including (in addition to PDs) civil and military police, and forensic and security investigators, and is not, therefore, a trade association for PDs. Both bodies have codes of ethics which, albeit necessarily generally framed, call for high moral, legal and professional standards among their members.

A second division is on the issue of whether PDs should be licensed by the State, as recommended by Younger (1972), an issue which divides members and non-members alike. Some see it as the only way of excluding certain 'cowboys' from their ranks, and thus raising the standing of the profession in the eyes of official bodies – it might also have a spin-off by increasing access to some data banks currently closed to them. Others fear that the conditions of the licence might worsen over time, that the profession might have its current freedoms curtailed, and that at worst, the licence might be revoked, leaving the individual out of work. Draft legislation promoted by both ABI and IPI has run into several difficulties (see *Police Review*, 26 November 1982). It has scarcely received the enthusiastic support of the Home Office.

Thus it is difficult for a prospective client to have a good idea of the quality of the PD who is being approached for the first time. The ABI and IPI have codes of ethics which they expect their members to comply with; but non-members may nevertheless have the most honourable, as well as the most underhand, among their ranks. There seems to be no way of having a quality assurance in advance.

Most PDs are involved in locating missing persons, though the vast majority of these cases come from institutions such as banks, finance houses or solicitors whose interest is debt collection. (For this aspect of the work, the PD should be licensed by the Office of Fair Trading.) These cases are so numerous that they are normally accepted at cheap rates, in bulk, so that only the cheapest and speediest methods can be employed to solve them. Debt has increased considerably during the recession, and about one and a half million cases reach the county courts every year. More are joining the ranks of the 'professional debtor' – one who deliberately accumulates debt from several sources, only to do a moonlight flit. Most debtors have to be located by means of various telephone calls – otherwise the work would not be a viable proposition. The other main problem with debt recovery, from the PD's point of view, is that many clients will offer a fee which is a percentage of the amount recovered; this arrangement has led some PDs to refuse such work.

The more genuine missing-person case, however, forms a very small proportion of most PDs' business – perhaps of the order of one or two per cent – except for a few who specialise in the work. Then most of the clients are spouses anxious to bring divorce proceedings, with others very occasionally – an adopted adult seeking a natural parent, for example, may number perhaps a couple of cases a year for a typical small agency. The client in these cases has normally no direct *financial* interest in the outcome, and many enquirers are put off by the fee quoted. The ostensible basis is either a retainer (perhaps £100) plus an hourly rate; or a basic £15 per hour. In either case, there would be 25p per mile travelling expenses, the rate allowed by the Inland Revenue. (I say 'ostensible' because more than one suggested to me that the fee depends to some extent on the client's apparent ability to pay.) The fees are significantly higher in the London area, where backhanders are reputedly more numerous.

It will be seen that PDs have a much wider clientele in relation to missing persons than the police (who will not search for a civil debtor), or the Salvation Army (who search only for close, adult relatives). When asked what missing persons case they would *not* accept, given the right fee, a small minority had refused to help a natural parent looking for an adopted child (one believing it to be illegal), but all said they would not assist if they detected criminal intent on the part of the client. This, of course, is sometimes impossible to judge in advance, and the instinct for self-preservation necessitates the development of techniques for inoffensive withdrawal from such cases.

Success rates in tracing most types of missing persons are claimed to be about seventy per cent, though much lower in a few cases, such as finding adopted children.

A wide range of sources, to be found among Section C, is used by the PD engaged on 'a trace'. Those open to the general public are not the most helpful, or the easiest to use, if the person has been missing for weeks rather than years, so legitimate (or, at least, not illegal) short-cuts may be employed. The public has no right of access to many records of local authorities, or banks, for example; but if such an institution has employed that agency in the past, and a relationship of trust has developed, then information may be exchanged. Solicitors, if clients, can also prove useful in acquiring information. One PD interviewed said he was able to buy new addresses of council tenants from some local authorities, at a fee which varied from 50p to £50.

Anyone in business, but not a private individual, can make use of the services offered by the United Association for the Protection of Trade (UAPT) of Croydon, and CCN Systems of Nottingham, an offshoot of Great Universal Stores. These firms carry computerised information about very large numbers of individuals. UAPT is non-profit-making, and open only to members of the Association; CCN sells data to anyone in business making an enquiry. Each holds the electoral register for the entire country (both being able to do a name search within each district) with individuals or addresses 'flagged' if earlier enquiries had been made about them. Payment profiles and credit checks are also stored, based on information fed in by private and public credit-granting agencies; 'missing' debtors are also flagged, so that creditors will be alerted if they try to gain credit from a new address; and all county-court judgements relating to debt and insolvency are recorded. CCN will also provide lists of shareholders, and itself operates a debt collection facility on a commission basis. If its data are insufficient to locate an individual, however, it will probably hand over the search to a detective agency.

Gaining confidential information by deception is not in itself a criminal offence; but sometimes an excess of zeal or the pursuit of efficiency leads some PDs towards forbidden territory; practices highlighted by the *Guardian* (11 May 1971), the Younger Report (1972) and Madgwick and Smyth (1974) still continue. Normally, they operate through a middleman employed in, or recently retired from, the institution from which data is being sought. A simple telephone call to such a middleman can still gain access to most data banks in this country.

More rarely, an attempt will be made to tap the information directly. On a normal 'missing-person' case, this is most unlikely to be done by hacking – it would not be worth the time even if the expertise were there. The information is sought via a direct telephone call, to which government departments *should* react by checking the identity of the caller, thus effectively blocking this route in. However, the vigilance of officials is not complete – checking the accuracy of a 'phone-back' number is not always done, for example, and the more ingenious PD will exploit stories of national interest, and times when more experienced officials are unlikely to be on duty, so that junior staff may be persuaded to pass information over the telephone. They are not alone in using such techniques, of course; the better known exponents are investigative journalists.

What distinguishes the really skilful PD from the merely knowledgeable, however, is the instinct for 'leg work' – the solving of problems by methods other than reliance on documentary evidence. It is this quality, albeit incipient, which marks out the few good applicants for an agency post from the other ninety per cent who think that a PD's life is all Philip Marlowe and James Bond. The ability to be inconspicuous if necessary, to understand and exploit other people's motives, and to work unsocial hours are far more important to a successful career. There is no glamour; but there can be a lot of satisfaction when a distressed client's problems are ingeniously solved. Interviewing the friends of a missing person, for example, is an obvious line to take but often more information can be obtained from enemies, from children, or from older or nosier neighbours, especially when they are interviewed alone – they are less eager to protect confidentiality. Persuading others to supply information is not always easy, and the PD has often to adopt another identity; announcing oneself as a PD to the friend of an absconder is asking for the door to be slammed in the face – but it may be done in the hope that an immediate warning telephone call on a previously 'bugged' line will reveal the absconder's whereabouts. Such equipment is available through advertisements in the national press.

Particularly useful is the device of indicating that it is in the financial interest of the missing person that he be found. Failing to disabuse interviewees who believe that the PD is a policeman because of his manner; searching a missing person's dustbins as well as his diaries; interviewing people on their own, without witnesses; all such methods may elicit facts unobtainable without subterfuge, in the interest of the client. Although the Data Protection Act was partly designed to safeguard confidentiality, it might have the effect of greater access through impersonation, unless holders of computerised data become more meticulous about identity checking especially after 11 November 1987.

B4—Bank trust companies

Bank trust companies become involved in searching for missing persons in two main ways. One of their normal functions is to act as executor to a will, either because they are named directly, or because all the surviving named executors ask the bank to act on their behalf. In so doing, the bank may be faced with problems similar to those of normal executors; (see pp. 162–3).

Difficulties in finding beneficiaries sometimes arise because the instructions of the testator are not sufficiently clear, and those problems are usually magnified when the will has been made many years earlier. If, for example, there is a legacy to 'the daughter of my friend Kathleen', or 'if my children die before me, to the son of Agnes Pritchard, my former housekeeper', then the executor will not even know the names of the beneficiary concerned, let alone his whereabouts. In other cases, it is the addresses concerned which may be out of date, or not included in the will itself, or among the testator's papers. Perhaps the beneficiary has changed name, or emigrated.

Again, the bank trust company can be called upon to act in cases of intestacy. Here, the rules governing the devolution of property are already laid down in a sequence starting with the surviving spouse and ending (where there are no relatives) with the Crown. Even at this stage, the Treasury Solicitor may formally advertise, and this is sometimes how firms such as Fraser & Fraser, George B. Hooper & Son, and Alfred A. Smith & Son, all of London, which specialise in approaching individuals out of the blue with proof of an inheritance from an unspecified relative pick up the information in the first place. (Other firms merely approach individuals with the right surname and sell the information about unclaimed estates whether the individuals are entitled to receive them or not.) 'Relatives' can include uncles, aunts, and the issue of uncles, aunts, brothers, sisters, and half-blood relatives; it is the job of the trust company to discover whether such relatives exist, and where they are. Often this is a simple task, and I have no wish to exaggerate the size of the problem – probably ninety-five per cent of beneficiaries are located without undue difficulty. However, it is always instructive to see how professionals set about finding the few awkward ones.

Few banks lay down either formal procedures or guidelines on how much to spend on the search, other than to ensure that the costs are properly incurred, and are not disproportionate to the sum at stake. Trust companies vary in the amount of time and expertise they can devote to the task themselves before subcontracting the investigation. After exhausting the information available through the immediate family, friends, or papers of the deceased, a wide variety of the sources listed in Section C may be tried. They also try advertising, either in the personal or public sections of the most likely regional newspapers, or in one of the nationals, especially the *News of the World*. However, more than one trust company manager has expressed reservations about this method, partly because it invites peculiar replies and even fraudulent claims, all of which have to be investigated. In addition, each respondent's antecedents have to be checked, with no guarantee that all or any are entitled to benefit, sometimes causing unnecessary delay and expense.

If these methods fail to locate the individuals, another agency might be called in to help – some have turned, with a degree of success, to the Salvation Army, though as indicated in Section B2, they will act only on compassionate grounds. Occasionally a firm of private detectives will be used, especially where the identity and a recent locality is known. Others commission one of the specialised agencies which advertise in the legal journals. Probably the best known of these is Title Research of London who, for many years, have brought to bear on such problems the skills used by lawyers, archivists, librarians and genealogists. Operating for administrators, executors, trustees, and solicitors (rather than for private individuals), the firm undertakes the location of missing heirs and beneficiaries. They use a far wider range of sources than the banks themselves, and claim a high success rate of ninety per cent. Many of the persons are found to have died, though sometimes their descendants benefit. The cost of their operations cannot always be predetermined accurately, so the firm has developed a variety of arrangements to suit different circumstances. Their longest case lasted three years; others are resolved much more quickly, but of course much will depend on the size of the estate or legacy and how far the bank concerned is prepared to eat into it.

Whether or not a firm such as Title Research is employed, a trust company is sometimes faced with a situation in which it does not know whether *all* potential beneficiaries have been identified – in some cases, there may well be over 100 individuals to be traced. Both the bank, and indeed the research agency, have to protect themselves against the financial implications of the later appearance of a genuine claimant once the estate has been distributed. Four ways of overcoming such a problem may be used. The located beneficiaries can be asked to sign an indemnity by which they promise to repay an appropriate proportion of their inheritance if such an event occurs; if there is a real chance that the missing beneficiary will ultimately be found, a sum may be transferred to a dormant account by the bank; an insurance policy might be taken out against the eventuality, at a premium which would be determined by the individual circumstances; and *in extremis*, a 'Benjamin Order' (a presumption of death if nothing has been heard of the individual, by anyone who would normally be expected to be in contact, over a period of seven years) might be applied for.

Perhaps I should add that, even at my comparatively young age (which may be found in the case of some authors on the reverse side of their book's title page) research for this book has persuaded me to make my will, with names and addresses of all parties concerned. Too often, inheritances are received by default by those who were unknown to, or even disliked by, the deceased!

B5—The Media

Access to the media can be a very cheap, quick, and effective means of tracing individuals who have no objection to being contacted. Almost the full range of missing persons may be found among letters and advertisements in various publications, from unknown descendants of some common ancestor, former school friends, relatives separated by adoption or simply by the drift of time – only the youngest are rarely if ever sought by this means.

The BBC can reach more individuals than any other single agency, their emergency radio broadcasts providing the most famous of missing-persons messages. This service is available in only limited circumstances. It must be on behalf of a patient who is dangerously ill, which must be confirmed to the BBC by the hospital or doctor concerned, and try to reach no more than two relatives whose whereabouts have been known with the last seven years. Other means to trace them must have been tried. Such a message is normally broadcast (before the Radio 4 news at 0700 or 1800 hours) in one of two forms:

> Will Mary Elizabeth Perkins, last heard of three years ago at Croydon, go to 128 High Street, Stoke-on-Trent, where her mother, Mrs Hannah Brown (formerly Perkins), is dangerously ill.

> Will Mr and Mrs Herbert Johnson, of Staines Avenue, Harrow, who are now on a motor tour in Devonshire, in a Morris Minor car no A1X 857, and who were in Torquay last night, return home, as their son, Walter Johnson, aged 9, is dangerously ill.

The BBC will accept other messages for missing persons, including appeals for witnesses of accidents, only from the police.

Independent radio stations have a somewhat more liberal approach, though the policy of each will be a combination of the Standard

Practices laid down by the IBA and the discretion which may be exercised by the managing director and programme controller. Once again, messages will be relayed on behalf of the police and the dangerously ill, but it is also possible that appeals can be broadcast for those in whose interest it is that they should be found – a solicitor or bank trust company seeking a beneficiary, for example. I know of no example, however, of a station which has accepted a paid advertisement for a missing person, an eventuality not covered by the IBA's Standard Practice.

Paradoxically, all radio and television stations (both BBC and Independent) use missing persons as part of normal entertainment programmes. 'Hot Line', 'Surprise, Surprise' and 'Christmas Contact' exploited the emotions generated by family reunions; three boys found their father after TV/AM carried their appeal, and local radio stations often broadcast requests for contacts with former friends and relatives. Among the poignant of all these reunions is that of natural parent with adopted child, but as far as I have been able to ascertain, it is always at the request of the latter (see p. 67). Additionally, of course, investigative journalists have to locate long-lost individuals for such programmes as 'This is Your Life'.

Probably the best known of these national broadcasts is that which Charlie Chester has run for several years, usually on a Sunday evening on Radio 2. Depending on the actual time of the evening at which it is broadcast, the programme attracts between 90 and 350 requests each week, approximately half of which are for re-establishing contact with missing relatives or friends. Unfortunately, only about twelve of these can be put on the air because of the limitations of time, and the producer estimates that a sixty per cent success rate is obtained (the replies are all routed through his office). In principle, they will consider all types of request, though after only one or two unfortunate experiences, some trouble is taken to establish the bona fides of those whose requests are to be broadcast. These should be addressed to the producer at BBC Radio 2, Oxford Road, Manchester M60 1SJ. Among the programme's successes have been the reuniting of a brother in the UK with his sister in Canada after a separation of almost eighty years, and the crew of a wartime Lancaster bomber who had tried for years to find one of their gunners with whom they had lost contact after the war: he was found within twenty four hours.

Though broadcasting will reach more people, newspapers carry far more attempts to reach missing persons, and can of course be read at any time after printing, in contrast to the once-and-for-all transmission of radio or television. The *News of the World*, with a current circulation of over four million, has run a missing persons column for over a hundred years. They receive about eight requests each week, and are prepared to publish photographs. No cases are refused 'within reason', and the editorial staff believe that they have a high success rate. In 1984, *Exchange and Mart* began its 'Missing Persons Link-up' column, a fortnightly list of requests for contacts with missing relatives, next of kin, friends and acquaintances, and has an extra section for maiden names, in an astute recognition that women are harder to locate than men. During 1985, stimulated by publicity concerning new ways of advertising for missing children in the USA, several other newspapers began to carry a similar column, some specialising in missing children.

Most national (and indeed some local) papers will not carry letters appealing for lost contacts because of their sheer volume, and anyone hoping to use them faces a bill of £10 and upwards, the standard fee for an advertisement. In moving to the personal column of the classified section, they will join advertisements from solicitors and bank trust companies attempting to locate beneficiaries.

Occasionally there are advertisements in the Press and on the air for a few voluntary agencies which try to advise people in distress, or put people in touch with each other. Best known in the former category is International Find-a-Child, started early in 1984 by John Tate, father of Genette who disappeared in 1978 and is still on Scotland Yard's long-term missing persons files. Based at 28 The Broadway, Rainham, Essex, it offers an advisory service to parents who find themselves in the same plight; it also acts as a pressure group on their behalf, and in 1985 organised a touring bus which visited many parts of the country to advertise for the whereabouts of missing children.

The Reunion Register also advertises. This is a list of individuals who wish to be put into contact with others, and it receives applications following press entries, and from the Citizens Advice Bureau. The address is 2 Milton Court Farm Cottages, Westcott, Dorking, Surrey RH4 3NA, and there is a nominal fee of £6.50 for clients to insert details of the person they are seeking.

Many local papers, however, will publish a letter enquiring as to the whereabouts of individuals, and a survey of such letters published by the *Manchester Evening News* (billed as Britain's biggest regional newspaper) illustrates the scale, nature, and success rate of this technique. Over a twelve-month period, 112 letters were published, from people seeking siblings (eighteen per cent), parents or children (twenty per cent) including two adopted children seeking their natural parents, more distant relatives (thirty-four per cent), friends (twenty-one per cent) and a few (seven per cent) with what appear to be basically genealogical enquiries. The editors believe that most people who write in are middle-aged or elderly, remembering those who meant a great deal to them. Such a column is also useful for restoring contact with former sweethearts – as has already been noted, few of the bureaucratic routes are sympathetic to this motive.

It does seem extraordinary that so many people have lost contact with such close relatives; equally it is hoped that the numerous ways in which contact can be re-established, demonstrated in Section C, can make reunion much easier than most people imagine.

It is unclear whether the above distribution is an accurate reflection of the letters coming in, or whether the editor was more sympathetic towards publishing those seeking close relatives. When published as 'Letters to the Editor', they seem to stand a better chance of being noticed than an entry in the classified advertisements. For a fortunate few, a reporter sometimes takes a particular interest in the case, and gives it more prominence in the normal news columns.

An attempt was made to contact all the writers of these letters living in this country in order to ascertain how successful their appeal had been, and about two-thirds of those contacted said they were pleased with the result. There is a very similar figure provided subjectively by a few journalists in being asked to guess whether it was worth writing to a newspaper for this purpose. Often, the newspaper does not learn of its own successes, though some of the satisfactory outcomes are eminently newsworthy. In most instances, of course, the paper will not know, but *Exchange and Mart* does not provide writers' names or addresses, only box numbers, so they will soon be in a better position to comment on a response rate.

Newspapers, of course, have a keen eye for a good story, and it is always worthwhile bringing any unusual feature to their attention so that prominence can be given. A six-month search for her father whom she had not seen for sixteen years by a bride-to-be living in Ashton under Lyne ended when the *Manchester Evening News* made it a front-page story on 18 August 1984. He came forward immediately, and was found to be living in the same town.

In the USA, advertising has now gone to more extreme lengths, as parents have pictures of their missing children printed on to milk cartons. Here, only the police have circulated large numbers of posters in a similar effort, and that is often when foul play is suspected. Perhaps in this country, newspapers would be prepared to publish photographs of the long-term missing, who are relatively few in number, in the same way as photographs of abandoned children.

C—Sources

C1—Birth

Before a child born in England and Wales is six weeks old, the birth must by law be registered by a registrar of births in the administrative area where the event took place. The public has the right to see a specified birth entry only in those register books which are currently in use; thereafter, those books are centralised to the local Superintendent Registrar, and maintained indefinitely; they go back to 1 July 1837. The rules governing the system of civil registration in England and Wales are currently under review; see *Efficiency Scrutiny Report*, 1985.

Each entry of birth shows the following information: the entry number; the NHS number (since 29 September 1939); the district and sub-district of registration; the date and place of birth; the forename; the surname*; the places of birth of mother and father*; the father's occupation; the mother's occupation (after 1985); the mother's maiden name; her surname at marriage, if different from her maiden name*; the parents' usual address; the name, surname, qualification*, usual address*, and signature of the informant; the date of registration; the signature of the registrar; and any subsequent change of forename for the child if the change occurred within twelve months of the initial registration. The name of the father of an illegitimate child (now forming eighteen per cent of all births) will only be entered if (a) he is present at the registration and agrees that his name should be entered; (b) an affiliation order naming the father has been issued (see p. 68); or (c) the father has acknowledge paternity by a statutory declaration. (Data asterisked introduced in 1969.)

The Superintendent Registrar maintains an index to births in his area which is open to public inspection. For a specified entry, there is no charge for this access; but for multiple or unspecified entries for which a search longer than five years in the indexes might be involved, a general search fee of £10 may be levied. Anyone can buy a certified copy of anybody else's birth entry; the current fee is £5, but this might rise in 1986. No-one should therefore rely on a birth certificate as proof of identity.

At the General Register Office at St Catherine's House, 10 Kingsway, London, the State maintains a parallel, but national system to which copies of the original entries are sent by the registrars. The same information is available on these copies; but the indexes are national, and open to the public with no general search fee; the mother's maiden surname is in these national indexes. The fee for each certificate is again £5, but this rises to £10 if the enquiry is made by post.

An abbreviated copy of each entry is sent by the registrars to the NHS Central Register at Southport (see pp. 50–8), which also has copies of the national indexes on microfilm.

The main problems of access, therefore, are (a) cost; (b) accessibility to the only publicly available national index (there are professional searchers who undertake this work); and (c) the occasional problem of not finding an entry in the indexes (see Rogers, 1985).

There will also be a midwife's report on the birth of almost all children; these come under hospital records. See p. 143.

C2—Patient records of general practitioners, dentists and opticians

Registering with an NHS general practitioner (GP) is voluntary, but almost everybody does so. GPs, dentists and opticians are normally self-employed but much of their income is derived from the NHS, either in the form of capitation grants in the case of GPs, or payment for work undertaken, in the case of dentists and opticians. The result is that an elaborate system of GP patients' lists is overseen by the Family Practitioner Committee (see pp. 50–8), the *treatment* remaining solely on the GP's own records, whereas dentists and opticians must send a record of treatment on individual patients to the FPC (dentists via the national Dental Estimates Board) in order to receive the appropriate fee.

The GP's main record system has remained unchanged since 1911 – the manila envelope EC5 (male) and EC6 (female), which contains the patient's full name, (changes of) address, date of birth, NHS number, and succession of GP's names with whom the patient has been registered. The envelope contains several other forms – treatments, previous medical history, immunisations and vaccinations, and so on.

Any one patient may have supplementary data also on file – correspondence, X-rays, and ante-natal records, for example. (For further details, see Benjamin, 1980; Drury, 1973; and Jones *et al.*, 1981.) A new EC5/6 should be issued following adoption, though some GPs have been known merely to score through the former name and substitute the new one on the same form.

The NHS dentist and optician will maintain similar non-medical data about each patient – name, (change of) address, and date of birth. Dentists make some attempt to collect the NHS number, but opticians do not.

A GP's records are the property of the NHS, and are centralised and destroyed when the patient dies. Dental and opthalmic records, however, are the property of the dentists and opticians, do not leave their possession, and are destroyed when the patient is known to have died or transferred to another practitioner; as deaths are not automatically notifiable, their files contain plenty of dead people's records. In contrast, when a patient moves to the list of another NHS GP, his EC 5/6 should be sent to the FPC, which will forward it to the new doctor. Thus no doctor, dentist or optician normally knows *to whom* a former patient has transferred.

Doctors in private practice own their own records, which can therefore be destroyed after the death or retirement of the doctor. In practice, however, patient files are maintained for as long as a doctor in private practice has space for them; often long after the death of a patient. The notes may be handed over to another practitioner if the patient changes doctor, however, especially when the doctor dies or retires.

As in the case of hospital records, the approach to collecting the NHS number is relatively casual. Most dentists make no significant effort to collect it, and very few members of either profession, or their secretaries, understand the number well enough to know if they have been presented with a forgery, or one containing a significant clerical error.

These professionals may therefore be of service to those wishing to contact missing persons only if they continue to minister to the health needs of those individuals at their new address; in that case, most medical secretaries would be willing to forward a stamped, unaddressed letter, given an acceptable reason for the request.

Divulging a home address, however, is a different matter, for it is regarded as part of the total medical record to which rules of confidentiality apply. The relevant professional bodies can impose sanctions for breaches of confidence – three psychiatrists were struck off for this reason in 1983 – and the Hippocratic Oath, almost two and a half thousand years old, contains the earliest known rule on such a matter. 'Whatever I see or hear, in the life of men, which ought not to be spoken of abroad, I shall not divulge, as reckoning that all such should be kept secret.' The 1947 Declaration of Geneva made this more explicit: 'A doctor shall preserve absolute secrecy on all he knows about his patient because of the confidence entrusted in him.'

As with other health-care professions (for whom, see Körner, 1984) doctors have guidelines issued by the professional body – in their case, the General Medical Council (GMC). This body (1985) lists eight general circumstances in which disclosure of confidential information may be permitted. Among these are statutory requirements, such as the reporting of any of the twenty-nine 'notifiable diseases', or issuing of death certificates, for example; for medical research which has been approved by the relevant ethical committee; and, rarely, if it is in the public interest which should prevail over a doctor's duty to maintain his patient's confidence – for example, responding to the police investigation a 'grave or very serious' crime; the interpretation of 'serious' remains in the judgement of the GP concerned. The GMC guidelines apply to National Health and private practice doctors alike.

Two further qualifications. Those in physical charge of the GP's records are often the receptionists rather than the doctors themselves, and they are *sometimes* known to apply different standards to the release of information. In addition, it should not be assumed that everyone will have registered with a doctor. A study in Liverpool found that, of the single homeless in the city, only four per cent were registered with a GP (Brandon *et al.*, 1980).

C3—The NHS Central Register and Family Practitioner Committee Systems

The Office of Population Censuses and Surveys (OPCS) maintains, on behalf of the NHS, an index of almost all persons (a) alive in England and Wales on the evening of 29 September 1939; (b) born in England and Wales since that date; and/or (c) (re)entering the country and registering with an NHS doctor.

Information for this index is first generated by the registrars of births and deaths, and currently about 1,800 new cards are added daily. When deaths are recorded, the old cards are normally not destroyed, and the index has therefore accumulated about seventy-five million entries. Data is also received from GPs and Home Office immigration officers concerning individuals who are believed to have emigrated, and from several sources concerning change of name. The General Register Office (GRO) keeps it informed of adoptions (see p. 63).

Outside the GRO, this is the largest index of persons in the UK, and an astonishingly little appreciated asset to the NHS and to the nation generally. The manual, nominal cards are kept in alphabetical order of surname (there are plans for future computerisation), and record the following information:

(a) full name and (if since 29 September 1939), date and place of birth;

(b) NHS number;

(c) adoption;

(d) change of name (for example, at marriage, though the marriage itself is not recorded);

(e) the Family Practitioner Committee (FPC) with which the individual is, and has been, registered with an NHS doctor;

(f) whether the individual has been registered with an NHS doctor outside the FPC area – for example, in prison, or long term psychiatric hospital;

(g) if the individual is a registered cancer patient;

(h) if the individual is (potentially) the subject of certain medical research (see below);

(j) if the individual is believed to have emigrated;

(k) date and place of death.

(The DHSS was thus incorrect in its written evidence to the Franks Committee in stating that addresses are held on this index.)

Some cards are 'flagged' – that is, they are so marked that when an event (especially death) occurs to that individual, a medical research project which has expressed an interest can be alerted. Such research is carefully approved and monitored (see below).

FPCs supervise, maintain and administer the Family Practitioner Service in each of the District Health Authorities in the UK. They are responsible for, *inter alia*, recording patients on GP's lists, change of

GP, and change of area by NHS patients. FPC records are the main facilitating mechanism for determining the income of GPs from capitation fees. Most FPCs maintain a manual, nominal card system which is updated by the NHS Central Register, by registrars of births and deaths, by GPs, and by individuals, as well as the FPCs' own clerks. A few FPCs are adopting a computerised Master Patient Index system, developed at Tayside in Scotland, which also incorporates non-clinical hospital records of patients, some of whom will be registered with a doctor outside the district. The normal FPC index contains all patients living in their District no matter with which NHS doctor they are registered. Presumably, if the present basis for paying GPs were to be replaced by a voucher system, the patient index would still have to be maintained.

The FPC manual cards are kept in two sequences. One is in alphabetical order of surname, and records:

(a) full name of patient;
(b) the NHS number;
(c) current and former addresses;
(d) the doctor with whom the patient is registered;
(e) change of FPC;
(f) date of dath.

The FPC is involved in the process of recording adoption (see p. 63), but forwards the original card to the NHS Central Register at Southport. If a patient leaves the area or dies, the card is maintained for up to three years (the length depending on the storage space available in each office), and is then destroyed. However, if a Master Patient Index (or 'Community Index' in its more colloquial form) is used, the record will probably be kept indefinitely.

A separate register is maintained, listing patients against each doctor, and divided into three age groups (under sixty-five; sixty-six to seventy-four; seventy-five and over) which relate to different rates of pay to doctors applicable to different ages of his patients.

Even with this fairly tight administrative control, the number of patients registered with doctors is believed to be over ten per cent higher than the total population. This phenomenon, known in the trade as 'inflation', is caused by some patients registering with more than one doctor (for example, holiday-makers, students), and also by delays in withdrawing from the lists those who have emigrated or died. The rate of inflation varies, of course, from one FPC to another.

As indicated at the start of this section, almost all people alive in

England and Wales will have been issued with an NHS number, though during the War this will have been their National Identity number. For those born and living in this country since 29 September 1939, it is the only number which stays with that person from birth to death and as such it is, *prima facie*, the most likely to be useful as the basis for any scheme of record linkage – not only within the NHS system, but across government departments and even private institutions. There is no practical reason why the NHS number could not replace National Insurance, premium bond holder, or mortgagee reference numbers, for example.

Within the NHS, it is used as a basis for ensuring that GPs are paid according to the number of patients on their lists by identifying each with a unique number; it also establishes a patient's right to treatment under the NHS. More than any other available data, it allows the system to distinguish one John Smith from all the others, and to record his movement from one doctor to another.

The number itself has a simplicity of design which has now proved effective for almost five decades. The enumeration of 29 September 1939 ascribed a unique, four-letter code to areas believed to contain fewer than one thousand households, each being given a numerical figure less than 1,000. Within each household, individuals in that house were given a further numerical figure according to their place in the family, this second figure being separated from the first by a stroke or colon. For example, NWRP was a code for an area which included Prestwich, north of Manchester; 228 represented a household at 230 Butterstile Lane; and /3 was the eldest (in fact the only) child living with two parents. The first letter indicates a broad idea of area, any starting with A, for example, being in London, S in Scotland, U in Northern Ireland, and Z in Wales. Many children were taught to recite their number during the War, and some wore it on a necklace which, ironically enough, caused a few fatal accidents.

Those born since 29 September 1939 have been given a number by a registrar of births, in a chronological sequence relating to place and date of registration, rather than a number relating to the family concerned. The stroke or colon was abandoned, and until 1 January 1965 all live births registered were given a four-letter area code and a numerical figure less than 1,000, in a chronological sequence. These area codes are not published. They changed slightly in 1939, and more significantly in 1947, 1956 and 1965, with the period 1956–65 being much more difficult to interpret than the system designed to baffle the enemy during the Second World War. If your NHS number is DQWV 213, please contact Manchester University Press, where you will learn something to your advantage.

The present five-letter codes were introduced in 1965, the first two letters representing the registration district, the third the sub-district or registration officer involved, and fourth a year code, and the fifth a quarter-year. Some codes changed at the time of local government reorganisation in 1974. As the fourth letter (year code) has now gone almost through the alphabet, 1986 being represented by X, the series will have to change again before the end of the decade, at which point the principles on which it is based may be altered more radically than ever before.

Irrespective of the political and ethical arguments against using any number to link medical, let alone non-medical, records, I think that the NHS number may no longer be suited to its purpose. There is, of course, a lack of awareness among the general public as to the meaning of the number – ask the man in the street for his NHS number, and the odds are that he will give you his National Insurance number instead. Many lose their medical card (which is normally the only document in their possession on which the number is given), and it is common to enter and leave hospital without providing it. One hospital surveyed for this book had no space for the number on its admission form, and indeed the first Körner report (Körner, 1982) recommended, albeit 'regretfully', that hospitals should no longer record it. The consequences of not supplying the number (for the patient, the doctor, or the hospital administrator) appear to be nil, and different parts of the 'National' Health Service have now evolved different schemes for patient identification – see, for example, the Section on health visitors' records (C18).

The number is not only easy to lose; it is also prone to error in transcription, and very few people in the NHS, let alone among the general public, are sufficiently knowledgeable to be aware that it has happened. My guess is that every GP has patients registered using incorrect numbers, some of them indeed impossible numbers. Furthermore, as entries on the medical card are easily removed and replaced, a black market in them has developed because agencies such as the Post Office accept the cards as proof of identity, against the best advice of the NHS, for it makes it possible to maintain more than one identity for personal gain. Most FPCs make a note on the Medical Index card if a replacement is requested, in order to pinpoint anyone who makes a suspiciously high number of such requests.

Even without forgery, anyone claiming to be a new entrant into the NHS patient registers will be given a new card with an allocated number (though not without the advice of the relevant FPC). Again, although the number is permanent for most people, it has been legitimately changed for some – for example, those who served in the War abroad will have three letters and seven digits; those who lost their card during the War will have been issued with a new number starting with the letter Y; many who, since 1952, have been adopted; and those who have asked for their number to be changed because there is something unfortunate about it. Also, it cannot be used at all for children before their birth has been registered, when they are up to six weeks old – yet they are probably already being treated by the NHS.

These objections to using the number as a more generalised way of identifying individuals, even within the NHS, could be overcome relatively simply; but the most serious defect could not have been foreseen by its designers in the 1930s, whose prime object was a number which could be used at short notice for security and rationing within the technology then in use. It is the relentless spread of computerisation, untrammelled in this case by the Data Protection Act, which more than anything else may cause the phasing-out of the present system of coding, though it should be said that the subject is a matter of some controversy within the NHS. (See, e.g., *British Medical Journal*, 15 December 1973, 674.) As has been noted, the number is prone to error in transcription, and the standard way in which a computer can be programmed to eliminate such errors is by the use of a check digit. To adapt the present system of NHS numbers so that they can be effectively computerised would necessitate them being rewritten to make them of equal length, translating letters into numbers at the same time. The effect would be to double its length from the present seven-slot or eight-slot to a minimum of fifteen, the same as the unwieldy and very forgettable gas, electricity or water board reference numbers. Despite this, some FPCs are basing their computerised identification system on the NHS number.

To learn the NHS number of anyone born in this country since 29 September 1939 is very simple – it is on a copy of the individual's short birth certificate, if bought from a superintendent registrar. Medical researchers may also be able to obtain it from copies of the full birth entry kept by the NHS Central Register, if their research has been approved. To learn the number of anyone already alive on that date in 1939 is impossible unless you have access to:

(a) their address on that date, plus the original enumeration returns – effectively, this is restricted to certain OPCS personnel;

(b) the number of some other person at that address and the knowledge of who else lived there at that time; or

(c) an NHS document on which it is recorded.

The NHS Central Register also keeps a cross-reference system so that most people who are given a replacement number can be traced.

It is not obvious why anyone would wish to acquire the NHS number of a missing person, when it is clear that most people in the NHS do not even use it. The use of the Central Register for tracing missing persons is almost entirely confined to authorised medical research, and those interest in this aspect are directed to the pamphlet *The National Health Service Central Register as an aid to medical research* which, together with the appropriate application forms, is obtainable from the Chief Medical Statistician (Dept MR), Medical Statistics Division, St Catherine's House, 10 Kingsway, London WC2B 6JP. The aims, methodology, and arrangements for security and confidentiality must be approved by the OPCS and the BMA. Once a project has been agreed, a charge is made for the service of identifying the subjects of the research, and it is about fifty per cent cheaper if the NHS numbers of the individuals can be provided by the researcher.

Research programmes involving only one district health authority can be received by the local Medical Committee, which would then operate as appropriate through the FPC and/or GPs. In this case, knowing the NHS numbers would still be useful, though not as important.

For many investigations (tracing all former employees of a chemical works, for example), both tiers – the Central Register and FPC – have to be used in conjunction with each other because individual addresses or GPs are not recorded by the former, and the latter cover only a small geographical area. If the likely, or recent, whereabouts of the missing person(s) are known, the first approach should be to the administrator of the local FPC – the address will be found under the District Health Authority entries in the phone book. If their approximate whereabouts are not known, the Central Register at Southport should be used.

Each of these two tiers act independently of each other, and put severe restrictions on the reasons for which they are prepared to provide help. Both limit access even within their own staff, unauthorised disclosure of personal data being an offence punishable by dismissal. The Central Register is maintained by Civil Servants, who are subject additionally to Section 2 of the 1911 Official Secrets Act, though it has never been used in their case.

Basically, therefore, the system is accessed only by those who have an interest in the medical health of the individuals concerned, or in that of the community, a district medical officer, for example. As noted by Rule (1971), it can also be used by the police in trying to solve a serious crime, though many FPC administrators are unwilling to provide such help without a court order. The Secretary of State, in a written reply to a Parliamentary question in 1970, stated that some information about an individual can be divulged without his consent if it was in his own interest, if it was in the public interest, or if there was a statutory requirement to do so. (This may soon be enshrined in legislation.) Addresses may also be divulged to court clerks in affiliation or maintenance cases.

However, even though information will not be given to anyone other than the above, the system can also be used as a channel of communication with a missing person in certain circumstances. If you wish to contact an individual for reasons which are clearly in his financial interests, or in the medical interest of himself or others, you can apply to the Administrator of the Central Register (or FPC if known) setting out the relevant details and enclosing an unsealed letter to the individual concerned. It is probable that the Central Register would act only in response to a solicitor, bank trust company, or insurance company, and of course would have to forward the request to the relevant FPC which would know the individual's address. Letters would not be forwarded in cases of adoption, however.

FPC administrators, not being Civil Servants, are *able* to take a somewhat more liberal view of such requests, while retaining the same principles of confidentiality. Such letters, unsealed and with an explanation, would again be forwarded for medical or financial reasons, and also for simple family contact upon request from individuals as well as from organisations such as the Salvation Army. Some administrators prefer to approach the 'lost contact' themselves and explain that their whereabouts are being sought – it is then up to the individual to respond. Other administrators, however, take a much harder line, and are unwilling to give even this amount of help as time and compassion would allow, arguing that their records should not be used for this purpose. It is also clear that, whatever attitude is taken currently, FPC administrators would not offer this service if the number of requests rose sharply.

Finally, it should be added that, even if the facilities of these two NHS systems are available, there is still no guarantee that contact can be made with the missing person. As with so many other indexes, they are of little help in locating runaway juveniles; and medical research teams report that, all too often, the addresses provided are out of date. Acheson (1967) quotes two studies which failed to find 14.4 per cent and a staggering 48.3 per cent respectively at the addresses on the FPC files; Newhouse & Williams (1967) found 37.3 per cent of former employees of an asbestos factory, whose addresses were not known to Central Records of the DHSS (see pp. 94–9), by using the NHS Central Register. There was a discrepancy of between twenty per cent and forty per cent between the NHS and school records in Tayside in 1975, and twenty-five to fifty per cent between NHS and addresses on the electoral register (see Angus *et al.*, 1978).

C4—Baptism

Baptism is a voluntary religious ceremony conducted by most Christian denominations, Quakers being among the few exceptions. Non-Christian religions usually have an equivalent naming ceremony during the early weeks or months of life, though relatively few Hindus now seem to carry on the tradition of recording and guidance involving a guru in India.

Each religion – indeed, each sect – decides for itself what data to place on permanent record. Anglicans, for example, now record dates of birth and baptism, names of child and parents, address, occupations of both parents, the names of the godparents, and that of the minister performing the service. Roman Catholics record all the above (with the exception of occupations) and in addition the date of subsequent confirmation, and the date, parish and spouse when the child grows up and marries.

With the exception of the Anglican registers, all baptismal records in England and Wales are private documents, access to them being in the hands of the priest or individual record holder. I know of no index to *modern* entries which embraces more than a single parish, or which covers more than one denomination.

Anglican registers are governed by the 1978 Parochial Registers and Records Measure, and belong to the Parochial Church Council. A few modern registers, together with most whose most recent entry is more than a century old, are centralised to the local Diocesan Record Office, where it (or a microfilm copy) can be seen free of charge. If the register remains in the church, however, a search fee of £3.50 for the first hour, and £2.50 for each subsequent hour, is payable. Whether centralised or not, the public does have the right to search Anglican registers, provided it is at a reasonable time of day.

It should be added here that, if the denomination of a missing person is known, and the enquiry is not one to arouse suspicion, clergymen are usually very helpful in trying to locate individuals in their parish, or in discovering whether parishioners have moved.

C5—Adoption

Well over three-quarters of a million people have been adopted in England and Wales since the legal process was first established on 1 January 1927; any 'adoption' before that date would have been, *de jure*, a fostering, and the section which follows does not apply to them. There continues to be some relationship in law between the natural family and the adopted child, and the personal urge to re-establish contact, particularly marked if the children are not brought up in the knowledge that they are adopted, or after the death of the adoptive parents, leads to some of the most poignant 'lost contact' stories (see Toynbee, 1985).

There are three separable problems. How can anyone tell whether they are adopted or not? Oddly enough, it is much easier to discover that you are adopted than to know that you are not, because of the difficulty of recognising normality when you are not familiar with the abnormal. Suspicion by teenagers that they are adopted – 'how can *they* be my real parents?' – is very common. Secondly, how is adoption recorded, and who has access to the records which show the identities of both natural parent and adopted child? Finally, once adopted children learn their original identity, how can their natural parents be located if they are not at the address on their birth certificate? Such answers as can be given to the first and third of these questions can best be understood by answering the second.

Adoption arouses a wide spectrum of emotions among those directly involved, including curiosity about the child's background (if not already known), and about such matters as religion, colour of eyes, IQ, state of health, and so on. Once the adoption order has been granted, the change of lifestyle and responsibilities, and the development of new personal relationships are rightly paramount. What is not evident to the new parents, or indeed to the old, is that an extraordinarily long sequence of records is created bureaucratically, behind the scenes.

Adoption orders can be granted by Domestic, County, or High Courts, but their documentation is essentially alike. Application to any of these can be along one of three routes, though in each case the local authority must be informed of the intent. Close relatives of the child can apply direct. Most adopted children have been born illegitimate, and if the mother subsequently marries a man who is not the child's father, it has been common for such a couple to adopt the child. (If the stepfather alone had done so, it would have removed the maternal rights from the mother!) In recent years, however, some courts have been far less inclined to grant adoption orders in these circumstances, and there are now substantial differences of approach from one part of the country to another (see Masson, Norbury & Chatterton, 1984).

Adoption societies, which must be approved by the DHSS, act to arrange adoptions for children who have little or no genetic connection with their adoptive parents. Their records, preserved for a minimum of seventy-five years, include the applications from both parties, the original birth certificates, the case notes, medical reports, and the outcome. They may also include the names of fathers of illegitimate children, even though these were not shown on the birth entry. A social history of the child's background is compiled, and a copy given to the adoptive parents for the child itself when it is older. Access to the information in adoption society files is available to the society's officers, DHSS inspectors, any guardian *ad litem* appointed by the court to see that the best interests of the child are paramount, and reporting officers; later, the adoptive parents, but only to confirm any information which they themselves had supplied; and also the adopted child, once having reached the age of eighteen (see later).

Thirdly, local councils can act as adoption agencies, normally delegating the function to their social services department: they act under the same regulations as adoption societies. They have similar records, and give similar access as the adoption societies. Additionally, however, access should also be given to any elected member of the full council if pursuing legitimate council business (following a ruling in the House of Lords in 1983; see *The Times*, 2 February 1983). I suspect that most social services departments would nevertheless use a variety of tactics to contrive to deny them this right, if at all possible. Access to records described so far is laid down by the Adoption Act (1958), the Children Act (1975) and the current Adoption Agency Regulations. It should be said, however, that the picture in reality may be somewhat different. Some of the records of the older societies have long since disappeared or have been destroyed, as indeed may the societies themselves. In those cases, it is possible that the local social services department has taken them over. At the time of local government reorganisation in 1974, even some local social services adoption files were lost. Adoption agencies do not normally keep in touch with either party for long after the hearing, so that the addresses on file can rapidly become out of date.

The courts themselves preserve records of cases prior to 12 November 1975 for a minimum of seventy-five years, but for only thirty years for later cases. The files include the application forms from both parties, the consent forms from children over the age of eight, and from the parents; medical certificates; original birth certificates; details of any maintainance orders, which are then cancelled; reports of any guardian *ad litem* (who is normally a social worker from another area) and reporting officers; the judge's notes on each case; and the outcome, including any conditions imposed. Very rarely, conditions can give access to the child by natural relatives, though with one reported exception, never the natural parents.

The adoption order itself is the authorisation for a child, whose original name, date of birth and sex are provided, to be adopted by parents whose names, address and occupation are also shown. It is also an order to the Registrar-General to make an entry in the Adopted Children Register, and to annotate the child's original birth entry.

Access to the court files is governed by Rule 32 of the Magistrates' Courts (Adoption) Rules (1984) or equivalent for other courts, and is available to the judge on the case, court officials, and 'birth counsellors' acting on behalf of adopted children once they reach the age of eighteen. Adopted children, parents, or adoption societies have no right of access, so it would be at the discretion of the judge or magistrate to give leave of the court.

An abbreviated copy of the order is given to the adoptive parents who, since 1958 at least, are normally given the right to know who the natural parents are (and even to meet them), a right which seems to be founded on good practice rather than on statute. The identity of the natural parents is shown on the application form and on the full adoption order. The full order is sent to the General Register Office, which thus becomes the third institution to know both the original and the new names of the children. It is quite common for some element of the original forenames to be incorporated into the new names of very young children – indeed, some adoption societies have asked for any original name given in baptism to be retained in the new identity. Older adoptees, of whom there are now an increasing number, usually keep theirs anyway.

From the data on the adoption order, the Registrar-General compiles the Adopted Children Register, which is maintained at Titchfield in Hampshire. A certificated copy of an entry from this register shows the district and sub-district of birth (which, if not known, is given as the place of adoption), new name and surname, the names, surname, address and occupation of the adoptive parents, the date of the order, the name of the court, and the date and reference number of the entry. Any person can buy a copy, the fee being £5, but no person outside a few GRO officials may see the register itself, or have access to the index which connects each entry to the original birth.

The Registrar-General does make available to the public, on the open shelves at St Catherine's House, 10 Kingsway, London, the index to the Adopted Children Register, which shows the new name, the year of birth (rarely entered before 1946), the date of the entry (only before 1966) and the volume/entry reference number. This number has been issued in a chronological sequence (with a break during the Second World War), and there are usually 500 or 1,000 entries in each volume.

The original birth entry is then marked 'Adopted' in the margin on both Superintendent Registrar and GRO copies (occasionally with the date of the order). This can subsequently be altered to 'Re-adopted' if appropriate, or the note scored through altogether if, for example, the child returns to its natural parents. A full copy of the entry, when purchased, will also have that annotation in the margin, but a short copy will not.

A short version of the adoptive certificate is also available. The short birth certificate was introduced in 1947 for the benefit of anyone who did not wish the names of the parents to be shown. It shows only the new name, and the date and place of birth, exactly as on a short certificate for a child not adopted, but with one significant difference (see below).

If issued before 1 April 1959, it will contain only the country of birth, not the place, and the earliest versions of short certificates, post-1947, do not give even this information.

The Registrar-General now passes details of adopted children to the NHS Central Register in Southport, (see pp. 50–8) where a file is created in the new name. The functions of the NHS Central Register with respect to adopted persons are to enable the Family Practitioner Services to operate without having to provide the link between the new and old identity. As at Titchfield, there is an index which relates each adopted child to its original birth entry or NHS number, and this is kept under lock and key, accessible to officials only in the relevant section.

The adoptive parents may register their new charge with a GP under the new name, with information about the adoption. (An adoption agency will have issued a form to adoptive parents for this purpose.) The doctor should ensure that the FPC is informed (assuming that only one person in a thousand actually reads the instruction concerning change of name on the front of their medical card). The FPC also creates a new file in the child's new name, and cancels the old one. Because adoption is often preceded by a trial period of fostering, the GP may already know the child by its original name and NHS number, but should start a newly-headed file in his own records. Often, however, the GP will simply score through the old name and write in the new. Done on the assumption that the patients are not allowed to examine their own files, this practice can effectively nullify all the secrecy built into the system so far. Only if and when a document is received from an FPC recording that an adopted child has registered with an NHS doctor does the Central Register cancel any previous FPC acceptance and call in medical records for transcription to the new name.

If the adoptive parent submits the child's former medical card, a new one will be issued in the new name but with the old number, allocated at the registration of birth since 29 September 1939 (see pp. 50–8). However, if the adoptive parents do not have the old card or number, or if they wish the number to be changed in order to break completely with the child's former identity, the FPC will so inform the Central Register which will issue a new number. Some FPCs prefer to see a new number allocated. If a new medical card is issued (which only occurs at the parents' request) the information supplied and type of case therefore determine whether the original number is allowed to remain or a new number issued.

The child benefit section of the DHSS central records system at Washington may already know of the child's existence through claims by the natural and/or foster parents, and the allowance will already be paid to the adoptive parents during any fostering period. Adoption itself may therefore make no difference to the allowance, and no public authority informs the Child Benefit Centre of the court's decision. The file at Washington is based on the name of the claimant, not the children. If the adoptive parent informs Washington of the change of name, the child's original name, under which the mother might have been receiving child benefit, will be removed from the record. However, there is a procedure covering cases of youngsters approaching their sixteenth birthday whose surnames appear to differ from those of the parents: an enquiry is sent to the child benefit payee asking in which name the child's National Insurance documents should be issued.

This does not end, by any means, the catalogue of records in which reference may be found to the adoption of individual children. If it takes places shortly after the birth, for example, hospital maternity and/or midwives' files may perhaps show a discharge destination address different from that of the mother. Health visitors also change their files appropriately, and the District Health Authority will probably issue the child with a new computerised number. However, the trail already described is the main route by which the State processes and documents the legal transformation from one identity to another. The system was designed to erect a series of barriers between natural parents and adopted child. From 1958, adopted children, once they themselves became adults, have had the right to go to court to overcome these barriers, so that they could learn of their own origins. This facility was greatly improved by the 1975 Children Act (see below). The exercising of this right presupposes that the individual knows that he is adopted, as indeed the majority do. Certainly, since the 1950's most courts have stressed the importance of bringing up their new charges in the knowledge that they are adopted. What may be a social and psychological desirability, however, is not a legal necessity, and no-one is compelled by law to tell children that they are adopted. Some still learn the fact when, as an adult, they need a passport for foreign travel, or go through the papers of their deceased parents.

In the context of the foregoing, it may now be seen how any person can tell, through documents to which access is possible, the fact of adoption. Application by adoptees for a full birth certificate in their present name will be fruitless through the normal indexes (though there are many other reaons why an entry is hard to find in those indexes – see Rogers, 1985). In the absence of a full certificate from the Adopted Children Register, there are four other documentary ways in which you may be able to learn of your own adoption, though only the fourth applies to everyone:

(a) Following adoption, children can be (re)baptised in their new name. Since the Adoption Act of 1958, such a baptism should describe the child as 'the adopted son/daughter of. . . .' However, because the tenor of this Act was to amend 52 Geo. III, c. 146 (George Rose's Act of 1812), I believe that this applies only to the Church of England. Whether this is strictly adhered to is a matter of surmise – the Anglican clergy are not renowned for a passion for administrative niceties.

(b) The DHA's child health file will have been replaced, and in some areas the new file marked 'Adopted'. One or two DHA officials have told me that they would confirm to persons under the age of twenty-five that they were adopted (at twenty-five, the file is destroyed).

(c) As indicated above, some adopted children are given a new NHS number on their medical card. This did not happen before 1952, so that for adoptees born between 1939 and 1952 the NHS number is a direct reference to their original registration of birth. It is possible to tell whether a new number has been issued, but only through a knowledge of the coding system, which has not been published. Since 1965, these new numbers are taken from batches allocated for issue also to immigrants and re-entrants to the system.

(d) It is ironic that, in the absence of a full adoptive certificate, the only sure way to confirm an adoption is by examining the very document which was designed to hide the fact – the short birth certificate. An adopted person can have a short birth certificate issued only by the Registrar-General, not by a superintendent registrar, and the reference number in the top right- (or bottom left-) hand corner will be an Adopted Children Register reference number, instead of the usual volume and page, or NHS, number.

Following the 1975 Children Act, adoptees between sixteen and eighteen years of age can apply to the Registrar-General for advice as to whether persons they intend to marry are within the prohibited degrees. (The full certificate, indicating adoption, would have to be produced by anyone intending to marry and being apparently under the age of about twenty-three.) For purposes of marriage, an adopted person stands in the same relationship to his genetic family as if he had not been adopted. Additionally, he is not allowed to marry his adopted parent, though may marry an adoptive sibling.

Once having reached their eighteenth birthday, adoptees can apply to the Registrar-General for a copy of their original birth entry. If the adoption was before 12 November 1976, and the applicant is unaware of the original birth particulars, this must be preceded by counselling, at the GRO, in the adoptee's current residential area, the area where the adoption took place, or in the area where the society which arranged the adoption is situated. It will be arranged by the Registrar-General, and is normally undertaken by a social worker known as a 'birth counsellor'. The advice given will be based on the individual case, after reference to the court and adoption agency records, and will enable the applicant to receive their original birth certificate. The nature of the advice is a matter for the professional judgement of the birth counsellors, though in the end they cannot deny the applicant a copy of the certificate. Applicants may also be given other information – for example, which agency, if any, arranged the adoption, and the address of the natural mother at the time of adoption, which might have been much later than the address of the birth entry.

Adoption counselling was given to 4,694 applicants between 26 November 1976, when the Act came into force, and the end of 1977. During 1978, this fell to 1,886. A total of 14,721 had applied before the end of 1983. More women than men apply, even though more boys than girls have been adopted. Many are women in their twenties, to whom genetic questions become important, or those whose adoptive parents have recently died. Many others have no need to go through the formal process at all because they already know their natural mother's identity. The reaction of most applicants on receiving a copy of their original entry is disappointment that it does not contain more information. A few may be spurred on by the acquisition of a name and address, though in practice, relatively few actually try to locate their natural parents. (For accounts of some who tried, see Toynbee, 1985.)

At this point, the search is almost identical to that for any other missing person, but not quite. There may be a couple of factors operating in the adoptee's favour. The Adoption Section of the GRO at Titchfield maintains a list of natural parents who have sent in a written expression of interest in being contacted by their natural children; so also do social services departments (who are, however, approached by some natural mothers wanting their children back as they approach wage-earning age!) It is up to the birth counsellor to decide whether an applicant should be told that the natural parent has expressed such a wish, and cases have been brought to my attention in which the clients have not been so informed.

Adopted persons tracing their natural parents can also find support from the latest and most successful of the voluntary groups which have tried to offer moral support for all parties in the adoption triangle: this is NORCAP (the National Organisation for the Reunion of Child and Parent) whose headquarters are at 49 Russell Hill Road, Purley CR2 2XB). In addition to offering advice, the organisation acts as a pressure group, but not as a tracing agency. Social services departments vary considerably in their approach to helping clients to locate their natural parents, and indeed in their ability to do so. (Usually, adoption does not take place in the authority where the natural parents live, unless there are unusually prescriptive circumstances – a condition regarding religion, for example.) As can be seen from the many local authority sources of information elsewhere in this book – electoral registers in alphabetical order of surname, for example – they may have access to information which is not available to the general public. Some authorities give as much help as time will allow; others give none. An additional useful role for the counsellor is to act as, or to arrange for a mediator to facilitate the first meeting between child and natural parents, and perhaps offer much-needed advice to the latter also.

Thus an adopted person may overcome the barriers erected by various bureaucracies in order to reach the natural parents. However, to a minority of the latter, the adopted child may be just as missing, and just as missed. In their case, the system is designed to resist all pressure from them to locate their children. No direct help is available from any of the institutions referred to above. So strong are these barriers that many natural parents believe, incorrectly, that it is illegal for them to try to overcome them, and relatively few actually try.

The ethical issues raised by this situation are quite fascinating, for they set the normal questions of civil liberty in the context of intense feelings aroused by family relationships. Most people are reluctant to give information or advice to support such a tracing, and NORCAP believes that natural parents should never initiate a search for their own children. Some private detectives will not accept such a client or, if they do, will not give the results of a successful search without the prior permission of the adopted person. It is generally accepted that the distress caused by the sudden reappearance of a natural parent is potentially much greater than that of an adoptee.

A cynic might ascribe an investigator's reluctance to accept these cases to the difficulty of solving them, rather than to any adherence to a code of ethics which does not really go to such a level of detail. Usually the only way to locate an adopted child is by utilising facts and memories which are in the possession of the natural parent – details of where the child had been fostered, details of the adoptive parents conveyed at the time of the adoption, and of course the date and place of birth, which can be related to various possible adoption certificates at St Catherine' s House. The Data Protection Act, confined as it is to computerised records, is of no assistance because the files which keep together the two identities of each child are held on manual systems.

Finally, the Children Act of 1975 extended the facility of access to original birth records only to the adoptees themselves. For other persons, trying to trace, for example, their natural grandparents, if the parent had been adopted, Section 20(5) of the Adoption Act of 1958 remains in force. An application can be made by any person to the court where the adoption order was granted, the High Court, or the Westminster Court (the last because St Catherine's House falls within its jurisdiction). I have little doubt that such an application would be sympathetically received by the court concerned.

C6—Affiliation orders

The name and address of the father of an illegitimate child may appear on its birth entry in certain circumstances (see p. 47). It is also possible that he was the subject of an affiliation order granted by a magistrate's court following an application by the mother or by the local authority social services department or the DHSS if the mother or child is receiving more than child benefit support from the State.

The hearing can be at any time between conception and the child's third birthday, and is at the court in the mother's home area. The mother must be single (i.e. without a husband who could have been the father).

The applicant completes a complaint form on which are recorded the names and addresses of the mother, child, and putative father; the onus is on the applicant to know where the respondent is living.

If the case is not contested, the order will be made, showing addresses at the time of the order, and the amount of maintenance payable. Copies are issued to both mother and father. If the case is contested, there will be a fuller record of the hearing, together with the results of a blood test which helps to establish the possibility or otherwise that the respondent is the father. The order will be cancelled if the child is subsequently adopted.

When the father subsequently pays maintenance at the prescribed rate and intervals, his address should be updated in the court record; missing defaulters may be referred to the police or civilian enforcement officers, who try to obtain his last-known address from the DHSS Central Records branch at Newcastle (see pp. 94-9), and subsequent correspondence may establish and record a change of address. The payments themselves, together with the results of further proceedings (e.g. to change the amount of maintenance), are computerised by many courts.

The payments may be made in first instance until the child's seventeenth birthday, at which point most of the file may be destroyed in order to save space. The court registers showing the basic facts from the hearing will be kept indefinitely, but many are not indexed so that it would be a long job to find one particular entry unless the reference number or month and year were known already.

Access to the data in these files is entirely at the discretion of the magistrates and their clerks – there are no written rules or national guidelines. Some will give the name and address of a father to a child who has reached the age of eighteen; others would only forward a letter to them. The DHSS, normally the only government department to make a request, is also given information; and all other applications – from relatives, the Salvation Army or the police, for example – are treated individually on their own merits.

C7—Student records

Records of school pupils are held by the schools themselves, not by the local education authorities (LEAs). It is the LEA, however, which establishes the minimum amount of information to be recorded in the schools under its control within the very general guidelines laid down by the DES in 1947 (Circular 151: Schools Records of Individual Development). Independent schools establish their own database, and LEA schools sometimes record more than they are formally required to do.

The pupil's file will probably contain full name, sex, date of birth (change of) address; names, addresses and telephone numbers (home and work) of parents or guardians; reports passed from primary school, the psychological service, education welfare officer, or from other advisory services; position of the child in the family (sometimes with the names of siblings, especially if these have attended the school); physical conditions of which the school should be aware, such as allergies, disabilities, or dietary requirements; the pupil's academic progress, subsequent career, education, and references for jobs. A separate book will record whether the child has received punishment during his school life.

It should be noted, however, that all educational establishments, especially in the schools sector, find it very difficult to maintain up-to-date addresses – even if former pupils return to the school for a visit, it is unlikely that they will be asked to update their address. Occasionally, though, it is possible to re-establish contact with individuals through these records, and at least one bank trust company was able to locate a missing beneficiary in this way, through an old boys' association.

Any attempt to record more information about home background is normally undertaken in the interests of the children and the way in which the school can respond to their individual needs, but it often relies on hearsay and therefore comes in for the same criticism as some of the data held on local police computers. Occasionally, this can be the cause of dispute or controversy – see, for example, *The Times*, 3 October 1975; the *News of the World*, 3 July 1977; and NACRO, 1984).

There appears to be no statutory minimum time for school records to be kept, though most LEAs give an instruction on this issue – the length varies considerably, the shortest to come to my attention being three years. Yet former pupils are likely to return to the school for a reference long after that period. Some, especially independent schools, keep their records of former pupils much longer, even indefinitely. Shortage of space is the prime reason for the destruction of these records. One of the schools approached actually published a list of its former pupils, with known current addresses, much to the consternation of one or two of them! All heads I spoke to were willing to forward an unaddressed letter to a former pupil, a minority requiring it to be unsealed, or preferring to contact the ex-pupil first to tell him of the enquiry.

Access to the data in school records is comparatively liberal. All teachers will probably be able to see the files on a 'need-to-know' basis. Some local authorities, such as the ILEA, have now given parents, and even pupils, the right to see their own files, though the data are normally held on manual systems and are therefore not covered by the Data Protection Act.

LEAs do not normally issue guidelines concerning disclosure of information from pupils' files – head teachers are expected to use their own discretion and common sense, referring only contentious cases to the LEA for advice. On the whole, I have found that heads do not have diverging opinions concerning good practice in this matter. The police are normally given access when it is seen to be in the public interest, and some heads prefer to do so before a witness from the staff. This information can be useful to the police who will wish to know the names and addresses of the friends of missing juveniles.

Other bona fide enquiries from former pupils would also be given the last-known address of a school friend; *The Guardian* (12 June 1984), however, reported a case in which a former pupil's photograph was given to the police, who then arrested him! If in doubt, the head teacher is expected to refer the matter to the Education Office, and their decision whether or not to divulge data is likely to be taken either on legal or on humanitarian grounds. The one situation which recurred during the interviews concerns the right of one parent to discover the current whereabouts of the spouse and child(ren) through the school records, and some LEAs have specifically forbidden heads to release this data. For detailed consideration of that, and many other, issues, see AMMA, 1985. The article calls for firmer policies by LEAs and schools, including the elimination of the hearsay material referred to above. See also *Police*, February 1986.

There is no central register of students in higher education – each institution, whether a college of higher education, polytechnic or university, designs and maintains its own record system, based on forms received at the time of application and registration. The data will normally include full name (including maiden name), home and term addresses, date of birth, marital status, sex, telephone number(s), name and address of next of kin, country of birth, sources of fees, previous educational experience, details of the course attended, and academic progress, with results and copies of references.

In the larger institutions, these records may be held in a duplicate system, the central register holding the official record (almost certainly on computer) and the department where the student registers keeping one of the parallel, manual records. Any computerised system is covered by the Data Protection Act, which (as in other walks of life) has had a limiting effect on the introduction of information technology. When interviewed for this book, some institutions said they were carefully deleting some of their computerised records of examination marks. Other sections recording the student's address might include the library, careers office, and student health centre.

Most institutions keep some basic student records permanently, perhaps on microfiche, as they never know when references and confirmation of awards (to a potential employer or professional body, for example) will be required in the future. These requests will be recorded, and this is often the only effective means by which a new address for ex-students will be ascertained. Some universities, conscious of this relative lack of contact with former students, are now creating alumni offices which will try to improve the institution's knowledge of future careers of its students. A substantial proportion of letters to former students – for meetings of the graduate body, or Convocation, for example – are returned marked 'Not known at this address', and in being allowed to examine my own record at one university, I found that the Registrar did not know my current address, but the library did.

All the institutions visited were prepared to forward unaddressed mail to present and former students; the request should be sent to the Registrar, and the envelope for forwarding sealed.

Access to information on former students is normally confined to the Registrar's staff, and to heads of departments. There are no national guidelines concerning confidentiality, though individual institutions or governing bodies normally have agreed procedures which can vary considerably from one to another.

The Home Office has the right of access because of the presence of overseas students. Attitudes toward other official bodies, particularly the DHSS vary, where the institution cannot be sure that the public good outweighs private confidentiality. All institutions approached gave data to the police on request, but an interesting exception may occur if the request involves an offence relating to the conduct of the institution itself. In 1984 lecturers at North London Polytechnic were prepared to face summonses rather than divulge the identities of students who had protested about the presence of another student on political grounds, and a High Court judge ruled, *only on pragmatic grounds*, that they should not have to do so. (In a similar way, a trade union will help the police with a normal criminal investigation involving one of its members, but not if the offence occurred as part of the activities of an official strike.)

Another location for records is the Students' Union, which will probably record full name, date of birth, year of entry, course, department, home and term addresses and telephone numbers, and signature. This will be kept on a manual card system, and is normally destroyed within a few years of the student leaving.

It is most unlikely that the Union will have recorded any data which is not more easily accessible through the Registrar's system, and Student Union officers are far more suspicious of requests for information from outside bodies, being particularly keen to protect the interests of overseas students. They are wary of authorities such as the police and the DHSS, preferring on the whole to deal with the Salvation Army, whose motives are understood. In all the interviews for this book, the only person who would vehemently refuse to give information to the police in a case such as that of the Yorkshire Ripper was a Student Union officer. Most would also help if they were convinced that any enquiry was in the financial interest of the student, but even then they would probably refer the enquirer to the Registrar. Their willingness to forward mail may depend on who you are, and the files are accessed only by staff in the general office and Union Executive members.

C8—Bank accounts

The overwhelming majority of adults in this country have a current bank account, each of which is numbered and associated with the name(s) and address(es) of the holder(s). The numbers themselves are allocated in a chronological sequence and normally incorporate a branch code and a check digit or other security device so that the bank's computer is most unlikely to process an erroneous account number. Cheque-card numbers are much simpler, often a chronological issue which changes on replacement; however, credit-card numbers stay with the holder permanently and contain a date reference for closing statements.

Although most have an account in their own name and address, the use of another name and/or address is not illegal in itself – only if it is done for a fraudulent purpose. There is no reason for a bank to record the fact that the same person holds two accounts at two addresses and I do not know any bank which asks that question; it would probably discover the fact only if the signatures were identical. The address has to be meaningful enough to allow correspondence (including new cheque books) to arrive. Some banks will allow their own address to be used for convenience and most banks invite new customers to record both home and mailing addresses, where these are different. The same person can, of course, have two accounts with two different banks.

In the 1960s and 70s, there was much discussion of the possibility of inter-bank co-operation through the development of networks linking not only separate banks but also a national data transmission system which would link computers with those of government departments (particularly the Inland Revenue) and large commercial organisations; see for example, Rowe, 1972. The LINK system is designed to connect some banks and building societies, allowing withdrawal of cash from automated dispensers. The possibility of electronic fund transfer between banks and major retailers is the most significant move now closer than the horizon, with Barclays, Midland and Nat West first in the field in England in 1985. Some banks do not even have a national computerised list of account holders; there is disagreement about the source of funding for the operation; and any massive computer system which would make the UK dependent on foreign technology arouses considerable suspicion.

Far from being the 'Big Brother' of the world of family finance, banks are themselves victims of bad debt on a scale the equivalent of one pound per annum for each account holder as a result of the theft and forging of the cheque-card system alone, which electronic fund transfer is designed to eliminate, and a substantial amount also results from civil debt absconders. The total amount of bad debt is perhaps a hundred times higher, amounting to about two per cent of the total loans. To trace the offenders, banks are as likely to engage the services of private detectives (probably on a percentage basis) as they are to use the facilities of other banks. There is a minimum of perhaps three figures below which a bank might consider that it is not worth the effort and cost to try to recover, though this amount varies from bank to bank. Equally, a determined effort would be made by the 'realisation' or 'recoveries' department of the bank if the debt is, say, in the order of at least four figures.

These are not the only missing persons in whom the banks have an interest. There are large numbers of dormant accounts – most being considered 'inactive' after a couple of years with no transactions and 'dormant' in three to five years, at which point the balance and the problem is transferred to the bank's central organisation. Little is done to find the rightful owners of these accounts beyond sending an annual letter to the last-known address. The reason for this is not necessarily a natural reluctance of the banks to find them; the vast majority of dormant accounts are so small that any significant effort to trace an owner would cost more than the amount of credit concerned.

When an account is opened, banks normally record the customer's name, marital status, occupation, signature and initial referees. Age is usually known but the Midland and the TSB record date of birth, which can be very useful for identification purposes if a common name is involved. The Midland, indeed, keeps a note of more data than the other big banks, including previous address of residence if at the present one for less than eighteen months; how long the customer has lived at his present address; home circumstances; employment status; how the customer is paid; and where the customer has banked before. It is likely that others will follow the example of the Midland when they introduce a credit-scoring system for assessing the credit-worthiness of customers (probably using CCN or UAPT). Most banks will know of change of occupation, as well as change of name or address. A bank might also have data on individuals who are not account holders – the Nat West, for example, will know the name, address, date of birth, marital status, bank and account number, employer, income, building society and name, occupation and place of employment of the spouse of anyone having a charge-card with Boots.

Computer file records are kept by each branch for as long as the customer remains there. When a cheque is issued, it is paid into the payee's bank and a note is kept for three years of the sorting code of the issuing bank and account to which the cheque itself is then returned. The cheques themselves, which are the property of the account holders who issue them, are kept for a statutory minimum of six years, after which they are normally waste-shredded. (I wonder what happens to the giant, publicity-stunt cheques which are a feature of competition pay-outs, or what would have happened to the cow in A. P. Herbert's famous misleading case?) Shortage of space may now be reducing this six-year period, and where 'cheque truncation' is practised, the cheques are not even returned to the issuing bank.

Thus your bank should be able to tell you which bank and branch was used by any person to whom you have paid a cheque in the last six years, so long as you can identify the particular entry concerned, and the bank, branch and account number from which a cheque has been paid into your own account for at least the previous three years. Another way to discover where someone else banks, of course, is through records of employers and any organisation such as the nationalised industries to whom cheques will almost certainly have been issued.

For banks such as Barclays, Lloyds or the Midland which have national lists of all account-holders, finding the current whereabouts of any one individual should be relatively easy, given a name and former address. For others, such as the Nat West, the TSB, or the former Williams & Glyn's, transfer could have been to any of the 3,200, 1,626 or 320 branches respectively (1984 figures), even assuming that the transfer was within the same company. However, a record of transfer is normally kept by some banks for as little as seven years, by others permanently. There would be no such record, of course, if the account had been closed rather than transferred.

All bank managers approached in connection with this book unhesitatingly expressed a willingness to forward, for anybody, a stamped, unaddressed, sealed envelope to any of their present or former account holders and would not require to know (though might be curious about) the reason for the request. It is evident that they already do this anyway – sometimes in an effort to locate bad debtors but often in order to contact someone who has filled in a cheque incorrectly.

Actual divulging of customers' addresses is another matter. Access to the records of any one branch is open to all officials working there but unauthorised, deliberate disclosure even of an address is a dismissable offence. Internal access to records of another branch, usually via a security-check system, varies from bank to bank; it is often not possible without both name and account number; and even then, the state of the account might be easier to access than the address. (The Younger Committee, which reported in 1972, seems to have been taken aback by the ease with which a customer of one bank can have a status report on the balance of a customer of another bank; this is still a daily feature of banking activity, for which there is only a small charge.)

Some outside bodies have a right to be given a customer's address, based originally on the Bankers' Books Evidence Act (1879); the police and Home Office with a warrant, the Inland Revenue, the Director-General of Fair Trading, and the Customs & Excise are among those normally listed in a branch-manager's manual as having such a right; the Inland Revenue, indeed, must be informed of anyone receiving over £150 per annum in bank interest. Following the collapse of Johnson Matthey Bankers Ltd in 1985, it seems probable that the Bank of England and/or its auditors will have increased access to individual accounts. I suspect that, in addition, most managers are prepared to help the police even without a warrant if the case is both urgent and serious.

Investigative journalists have successfully overcome the system which should deny them such access in a series of minor scandals, the most recent of which at the time of writing was that involving Mr Denis Thatcher and the *Sunday Times* (*Sunday Times*, 4 March 1984). I imagine that journalists have not been discouraged by the Press Council's verdict in August 1984 that the information had been obtained by 'justifiable subterfuge'. The subterfuge normally involves bank officials not adopting the normal 'phone-back' procedure when a telephone enquiry has been received, but sometimes it can be part of the 'old boy network' or a quid pro quo arrangement.

Private detectives used to advertise openly that they could obtain details of anyone's bank account. Their activities were reported to the Younger Committee, which was dismayed by the ease with which the banks' security could be penetrated. I have not found them advertising any more but the practice is still as prevalent and those with the right contacts do not need to have recourse to impersonation or even deception. Political parties have also been accused of gaining names and addresses from banks (see the *Guardian*, 29 and 30 March 1984, for example) though I really do not see why they should have to do so. (Lists of potential clients and customers can be obtained from firms such as Business Lists UK.)

Finally, access is sometimes requested by one joint account-holder in dispute with another and a bank's obligation is to *each* holder, not both jointly. For example, a deserted wife may wish to know from which branch her husband had withdrawn money from their joint account. In the tragic Lockwood case of January 1984, a husband living in Huddersfield was able to learn the approximate whereabouts of his wife from her withdrawal from a joint TSB account in London. The information would be provided but as soon as the manager knew of the dispute in question he would instruct any 'either-to-sign' to be converted to a 'both-to-sign' account, pending resolution of the problem. This, however, still leaves the bank open to receiving a forged second signature, so many managers would prefer to freeze the account. Although this might be difficult to justify legally, the bank would probably be prepared to take the issue to court for judgement and would still freeze the account as being the most reasonable action in dispute situations. Once an account is in dispute, banks should preserve the confidentiality of any new address from the other party, though compassion for one believed to be in genuine need might overcome an official's instinct to go by the book.

Many of the issues discussed above are left to the discretion of individual branch managers and in practice they will normally put the interest of the public good and the interest of the bank itself above the confidentiality of their clients' accounts and addresses, their actions being determined by common sense and good citizenship as well as by statute and the bank manual.

C9—Employers' records

A personal file on all employees is normally held from before, until often after, a period of employment concerned. The contents of this file are partly determined by the statutory needs of employers, but more substantially from their ever-increasing management requirements which vary considerably according to the size and complexity of the organisation. Normally your employer has more current information about you than any other record-keeper, and a large amount of it can be cross-referenced into other systems –

National Insurance, pensions, banks, the DVLC and so on.

Much of this information is recorded at the time of an *application* for a job, and the question of whether (and for how long) to store application forms for unsuccessful candidates is a matter of some controversy amongst employers – some firms do not keep any, others store them indefinitely for future reference, but most keep them for no more than two years. Even notes made during the interviewing process will now probably be kept for at least six months in order to protect the firm from later accusations of prejudice or bias, and can be the source of some embarrassment if they go adrift.

Application forms are regarded as confidential by employers, but are by no means always marked as such. (Only personnel records of central government departments are subject to Section 2 of the Official Secrets Act, however.) They normally contain full name, title, address, telephone number, date of birth, marital status, qualifications, previous posts held, and details of referees, with accompanying references, signature and date of application. Other data will be required for specific posts, but commonly include number of children, ethnic origin, disablements, and next of kin or emergency contact. Dyer (1979) reported that, of fifty different application forms for manual workers, only four of a total of seventy questions were common – name, address, date of birth and previous jobs. Once the appointment is made, the new employee will have added to this file his National Insurance number, the bank or (much more rarely) building society account (if any) into which a salary would be paid, the post and department, payroll number, starting date, tax code, in many cases trade union membership, car number and driving licence (especially if they are related to job or car loan), and medical notes of the firm's doctor, which belong to the firm, not to the NHS. For some professions, the file may be even fuller – teachers, for example, will have a copy of their service record card from the DES (Darlington Records Branch). During the period of employment, pay, deductions, absence and sickness will be recorded, and any references issued by the employer at the time of application for a new job. Following retirement, records of pensions paid will also be maintained. The statutory contract of employment does not normally include home address.

It will be noted that most of the personal details, except date of birth, National Insurance number, and ethnic origin, can change *during* the period of employment. It is in the clear interest of employees to inform their employer of some of these changes – improved qualifications might lead to increase in salary; failure to inform change of name or bank might result in non-receipt of salary. In the cases of banks or building societies offering mortgages to their staff, or of firms offering goods at reduced rates providing they are delivered at home, it is also important that the home address is kept up-to-date. However, no sanctions are involved for the majority of employees who fail to notify a change of address, and there is no compulsion on employers to provide an up-to-date address on the employee's Inland Revenue returns. One firm in my survey sent annual reminders about updating addresses, but had no means of knowing whether it was being complied with.

The payroll, or works' number allocated to individuals by their employers is normally unsophisticated, often carrying no meaning other than a simple chronological sequence. The most significant in the survey carried out for this book is the system used by a national retail company, the first three digits representing the branch, and the final five a chronological allocation; the last character is a digit in the case of salaried employees, or a letter (A to I and therefore the same length on a computer) for the wage-earners. Works' numbers may sometimes be used for identification purposes, with other institutions – for example on mortgage application forms; however, they are normally of little use outside the firm concerned, and might change if the individual changes department. The personnel number normally appears on clock sheets, pay slips, and now, notices of tax coding.

Some employers maintain records on both manual and computerised systems, the latter providing an extremely useful adjunct to, but rarely yet a replacement for, the former. According to *Which Computer* (August 1984) only fourteen per cent of personnel departments in the UK are computerised, the initial cost being felt to outweigh the return, and the Data Protection Act providing a further deterrent, unless programming is available which has the effect of undermining the spirit of the Act – part retrieval and printout of files, for example. The manual files are often in two forms, one a summary card, and the second a fuller folder which can become bulky with forms, correspondence, reports, reference copies and so on. When an employee leaves, the computer entry is normally wiped clean, the feeling being against storing computer tape because it implies having to store the hardware also. Additionally the Data Protection Act now prevents computerised data from being stored longer than necessary to the purpose for which it was collected. The full file is preserved on an internally agreed time schedule for periods varying from two to seven years or more; and the summary forms are kept much longer, sometimes indefinitely. The length is largely determined by legal requirements and the cost of storage. Many firms put their dormant personnel records on microfilm or microfiche, and this makes for longer storage times. (Indications are that current computer magnetic tape will last for about ten years, but it can be re-recorded.)

In a larger organisation, the full data on one individual is not normally found in a single location. Appointment, discipline and dismissal may be overseen by a personnel department, which maintains current files, and supplies management with statistical data to be used in decision-making processes; much material relating to pay will be kept by a finance department; pensions may be in a different section again, which should maintain notifications of death; and the semi-current and dormant system may be handled by a records management section. The most surprising thing to the outsider is the degree of suspicion between the various sections, personnel departments in particular being suspicious of intrusion because of the nature of the often delicate data which they hold. Information is divulged only on a 'need-to-know' basis, and even when it is fully computerised, access to individual elements may be separated by the use of different passwords. Elected councillors appear to have the right to see any local authority file, but would have to convince an officer that it was for part of his normal activity as a councillor. Internal security and access vary considerably between institutions. Monthly payroll printouts are commonly to be found on office desks showing name, works' number, department, grade, and National Insurance number, and one local authority visited produced a new microfiche list of employees every fortnight.

Requests for information about employees from outside bodies are not treated uniformly either by different firms or by departments within the same firm, and the right of disclosure is a decision of the individual institutions – or even individual record keepers – rather than any overarching body such as the Institute of Personnel Management. Most organisations approached in connection with this book, both public and private, were prepared to supply information to the police without a warrant, particularly if they were told the reason for the request – banks were an exception, as was a manager who had had unfortunate dealings with the police in the past. They would also be helpful to central government departments, though a few (both private and local government) said they would not supply such data to the DHSS.

The reaction to requests from non-governmental agencies depends on the agency concerned. Only a few private firms said that they would give the address of a present or former employee to the Salvation Army or to a bank trust company, but all were prepared to help by locating the individual and asking him to get in touch with the agency directly. All employers expressed a willingness to forward mail (for agencies or for private individuals) with no stipulation about whether the letter should be sealed or not. They might be curious about the reason for the request, but would not require to know it. It should be remembered however that even during employment, home addresses on file may be out-of-date; and most former employees do not have the courtesy to inform the organisation providing a reference whether an application for a new job has been successful. If the new address is kept only on computer, it is probable that the old address will be wiped off.

It is clear that most record-keepers feel that they need to protect employees from two groups of individuals in society – debt collectors and journalists – whose enquiries thus became more subtle/underhand in a vicious circle. Very few managers said they would listen to the reason for a private detective's enquiry and judge it on its merits. Nor do the interests of academic researchers – modern historians or sociologists – rank among the priorities of records managers, but the requirements of NHS-supported medical research receive a more sympathetic hearing. The computerisation of personnel records may lead to easier access by certain persons, given the technical knowledge, and patience in working out passwords. I believe, however, that computer storage is considerably safer than the old filing-cabinet system, a few keys for which would probably open half the cabinets in the country. This, however, is not how most enquirers operate – the way into the system is through the operator, not through the key or the password. As in so many other institutions, it is the plausible story, especially over the telephone, which will win through. Unauthorised divulging of personal data is treated by most organisations as gross misconduct, and may be punishable by dismissal. How many office staff can distinguish the ring of an internal from an external call? How many office juniors, during a lunch break, would refuse a home address to 'John, here, from Audit'?, Suspicions should be aroused, of course, if no 'phone back' number is offered; but how many check the telephone number actually given? See Buckland, 1985.

It should be stressed that the above conclusions are fairly gross generalisations. Larger organisations with formal procedures will nevertheless contain individuals with access to confidential data who are prepared to break their procedures if the case seems to warrant it. Most firms do not have such procedures – only precedent, the general guideline of 'do as you would be done by', and an unwillingness to live with the knowledge that a debtor, for example, was located through the divulging of an address. However, if managers are asked how they would hope other firms might co-operate in their own attempt to locate a debtor, the picture changes, and the logical outcome is the rise of the credit-rating company and the pooling of information on bad risks by, for example, insurance companies.

Ministry of Defence personnel records

Among employers' records, those of the Ministry of Defence (MOD) require more detailed attention; enquiries relating to them are frequent because of their number, the length of time for which they are kept, and the cameraderie among servicemen in particular. They are, of course, subject to Section 2 of the Official Secrets Act (1911), and may come under Section 1 also.

Generalisation about service records is almost impossible. Many older records have been culled at one time or another. Details of staff service, such as date of joining and leaving, and the particular arm or corps to which they belonged will always be found, but even details of postings might have been omitted on security grounds. The record will usually contain date of birth (or in some cases only age), education, physical description, and home address at the time of recruitment and discharge – any later address would be recorded only if there had been subsequent correspondence, though it could be obtained by the authorities if the person concerned was in receipt of a service pension. (The age of volunteers during the two wars was often supplied incorrectly, for patriotic reasons.) An individual's bank might be on record, though few non-officers would have bank accounts before the 1950s. Medical records are held in a separate series.

Each serviceman/woman is allocated a number; in the case of the Army, this has been issued chronologically and contains no internal coding – present recruits are given one containing eight digits. The possession of the number greatly facilitates the identification of the individual concerned.

The location of these records is quite complicated, and differs for civilian employees, officers, and other ranks.

Civilians

Enquiries about records of MOD (ex-) civilians should go to their last civilian management branch; if this is not known, the enquiry should go to CS(R)2f, Building 231 Nestles Avenue, Hayes, Middlesex UB3 4RH, where the file may be located, the relevant civilian management branch identified and asked to reply. Civilian records are currently held until the eighty fifth birthday of the data subject, and are accessed through the sequence department (e.g. Ministry of Supply), exact date of birth, and only then in alphabetical order of surname.

Army officers

Personnel records for all serving officers are held by the Army Officer Documentation Office, Government Buildings, Stanmore, Middlesex HA7 4PZ. When an officer becomes 'non-effective' (i.e., retires, resigns, or dies in service), the file is passed to CS(R)2b (Army Search), c/o Public Record Office, Bourne Avenue, Hayes, Middlesex.

Army other ranks

Each personnel file is held by one of the respective Manning and Records Offices, whose addresses are given in the published Army List (HMSO). It remains there for several years after the soldier has become non-effective, and is then centralised to CS(R)2b (address as for Army Officers above). Army other ranks records are accessed through the sequence regiment *from which discharged*, year of discharge, and only then alphabetical order of surname.

Royal Navy officers

Records of serving officers are with the Naval Secretary's Department, Old Admiralty Buildings (Ripley Block), Spring Gardens, London SW1A 2BE. Files of non-effective Royal Navy officers are transferred to CS(R)2a (Navy Search), c/o Public Record Office, Bourne Avenue, Hayes, Middlesex.

Royal Navy ratings
If the rating is still serving, or has only recently become non-effective, the record will be at HMS Centurion, Grange Road, Gosport, Hants PO13 9XA. It will then be transferred to CS(R)2a, as for RN Officers.

Royal Marines
Records are held at the Crafting and Records Office Royal Marines (DRORM), HMS Centurion, at the above address.

Royal Air Force
Enquiries should be directed to the RAF Personnel Management Centre, Innsworth, Gloucester GL3 1EZ.

The full records (all held on manual systems) are currently maintained for Army personnel who have been discharged since 1913, for Royal Navy personnel who entered since 1891, and for the RAF since its foundation. Older records are preserved permanently in the PRO, where any over seventy-five years old are open to the public.

Requests from the public for information from MOD personnel records run to some 3,000 *per month*, and relate to ex-servicemen's pensions, war medals, confirmation of service from various individuals and organisations, and genealogical research. Such requests are therefore normally met only for, or with written persmission of, the data subject, or next of kin, so long as the record keeper is satisfied as to the identity of the enquirer. Medical details will be provided only to a registered medical practitioner; qualified enquirers should therefore provide the name and address of their GP or other doctor treating them. It should be appreciated that this volume of requests is partly a reflection of the colossal volume of records concerned which, if proverbially upended, would form a pile fourteen times as high as Mount Everest. It has been estimated, however that each file is accessed an average of only once in its lifetime, when no longer in current use.

Ministry of Defence record keepers are normally willing to forward a stamped letter to a data subject, though as already observed the last known address (which will not be divulged) might be years out of date. There will be no requirement that the envelope should be unsealed.

There are some requests for information from institutions outside the MOD, and home addresses can be divulged to the police, the DHSS, the courts and in some cases to solicitors. Social welfare organisations, such as the Salvation Army, may be given more assistance than would be offered to a member of the general public, subject once again to the understanding that it is given in confidence.

The MOD has its own missing persons, who may be absentees without leave, or deserters. The relevant sections of the Army Act (1955), the Air Force Act (1955), the Naval Discipline Act (1957), the Army and Air Force Act (1961) and the Armed Forces Act (1966) describe the powers used to deal with such persons. Details of absentees (including physical description) are normally communicated to the civilian police (the latter on the PNC). There is no statute of limitation, so the record is maintained indefinitely – some are still available for the eighteenth century! The civilian police may arrest anyone suspected of being an absentee or deserter – indeed, in the absence of a police officer, so can anyone else.

C10—Unemployment records

National and local statistics concerning the numbers of people registered as unemployed are most conveniently found in the monthly *Employment Gazette*, the official journal of the Department of Employment (DE). At the time of writing, the level of these figures is only too familiar to most readers, there being about three and a quarter million (13.4% of the work-force) registered at the end of 1984.

It may seem ironic that it is this Department which processes claims for unemployment benefit. The arrangement by which the DE acts as an agent for the DHSS dates from an era in which the number of claimants was relatively small, and the DE provided an effective means by which each could be given a realistic chance of finding work, thus keeping benefit claims to a minimum. However, if the present high rate of long-term unemployment is maintained, there seems little reason why some of the responsibility for payments should not be undertaken directly by the DHSS.

Meanwhile, the DE has two main computer centres which hold British records of the unemployed. One, at Livingston, relates to claims made at offices in Scotland, the North, Yorkshire and Humberside, the north west, and part of the midlands; the other, at

Reading, relates to the remainder of England and Wales. Claims relating to long-term unemployed persons who are only required to attend quarterly, shore fishermen, and those claimants who are 'temporarily stopped' are not computerised, and their records are held only at the office at which the claim is made. The Government plans to install computer terminals at all benefit offices by 1988.

Unemployed persons are not on a separate number-identification system. The main heads of information on the records include full name, address, telephone number, date of birth, and National Insurance number (see pp. 95–6), which is deemed sufficient for identification. Family circumstances as provided by claimants are also recorded.

The records at the computer centre and the local office are normally retained for a maximum period of three years from the termination of the claim, but records relating to outstanding recoverable overpayments of unemployment benefit and those relating to fraud cases are retained for longer periods.

The DE is prepared to forward, without prejudice, a letter by ordinary post from an enquirer to any person whose address is known to the Department. If the enquiry comes from abroad or the enquirer is known to be foreign the letter must be unsealed. It should be sent to the manager of the DE office nearest to the last-known address of the individual concerned.

Access to the records at the computer centres is normally restricted to the unemployment benefit office dealing with the claim. However, under exceptional circumstances, e.g. suspected impersonation cases, headquarters or regional offices do have access to search facilities. The DE carries out the policies concerning confidentiality laid down by the DHSS, and will not normally divulge information without the written consent of the data subject (indeed, sometimes not even then). However, this general rule may be waived in cases in which disclosure is deemed to be necessary in the public interest, or in response to requests from a Clerk to the Justices or Registrar of the High Court relating to maintenance or affiliation proceedings.

Evidence from the DE to the Franks Committee suggested that the Department regarded the Official Secrets Acts as a useful safeguard because so much confidential data had to be handled by junior, often temporary staff, whose inexperience makes them vulnerable to the guile of private detectives. Somewhat surprisingly, that still reflects, apparently, the current situation.

C11—Voluntary associations, trade unions and professional registers

The grouping together of large numbers of individuals engaged in related occupations generates bureaucratic structures which normally allow movement between posts to be documented. It will probably be obvious from the nature of the work which organisation will be appropriate for employees – some occupations, indeed, are restricted either by statute or by closed-shop agreements. Generalisations about such diverse institutions as the British Medical Association and SOGAT '82 are not obvious, and there are indeed wide variations in practice even between industrial trade unions.

Normally such organisations record name, address, occupation, place of employment, date of entering the association, and signature. Salary will be known if it is related to membership fee, age if related to benefits, and academic, trade, or professional qualifications, if related to the nature of the organisation. The major difference between some professional organisations and others lies in their willingness (and for some, indeed, their statutory duty) to have their membership lists published. Names, addresses and qualifications of a large number of trades and professions can be obtained from current directories which may be seen in public libraries, many of them published annually (see Anderson, 1979).

In some cases, it is clearly in the public interest that names and addresses should be thus available, and in other cases it is in the interest of the members themselves. *Spotlight*, for example, is a shop-window for actors and actresses, with photographs, height, and colour of eyes. It is far from clear, however, why the public should not have the same access to the records of a registered health visitor in the same way that they have to those of doctors or public health engineers, yet I know of no organisation which, if it does not publish its members' names and addresses, does not regard the data as confidential.

There are other major differences between such associations. For example, some are entitled to receive data about their members from outside official bodies – notification of convictions (see Madgwick & Smythe, 1974) and of death. For the purpose of tracing missing persons, it is also important to recognise wide variations in bureaucratic practices, particularly within the trade-union sector. Most professional associations have a simple, centralised structure which holds the relevant data on all its members in one place, as do most voluntary societies. Trade unions, however, have a structure based on branch and region, as well as headquarters, the members' files being located and duplicated at different levels in different unions. USDAW, for example, maintains individual membership records both centrally and at branch level; in NALGO, however, they are held only at branch level, and SOGAT '82 holds them at district, not branch (chapel), level. Computerisation will probably lead to greater centralisation of records, with branches having terminal access to their own members only. It is partly because of this decentralisation of records that the names and addresses of branch secretaries are sometimes kept confidential by the unions concerned, even from other branch secretaries.

The organisation and purposes of the association may have a bearing on whether members' addresses, given at the time of joining, are kept up to date. Those with a centralised structure are more likely to hold a member's current address because there will be regular correspondence and journals which go directly to the home. Because the activities and lines of communication of many unions are based on the place of work, however, it is often the case that the home address is out of date in the records. Normally, this is of little consequence to the union concerned, though some, e.g. SOGAT '82, impose a small penalty on those who do not inform the union of a change of home address; and a cynic might observe that it was not in the interest of a working miner during the strike of 1984–5 that the NUM should have known his home address. This lack of up-to-date information sometimes makes the balloting of union members via their home address out of the question.

Most associations approached for this book expressed a willingness to forward unaddressed mail, and none would require that the letter be unsealed. Most unions made the point, however, that the employer was much more likely to have the current home address, and a few officials felt that it was not really part of their function to help enquirers in this way; some would prefer to contact the individual members themselves first and inform them of the enquiry. However, an association, especially of skilled persons, will probably keep the same members during several changes of employer, USDAW in contrast having a changeover of membership approaching 30 per cent annually. The 1.5 million strong T&GWU nationally would be able to locate an individual through its branch system if the name was relatively unusual, or if the membership number were known, but is reported to be compiling a national list of members, including home addresses.

The situation in many other unions is more complicated. Where membership files are held only at branch level, only the personal memories of other members, or the occasional record of change of branch would be able to help to trace the individual who had moved. In NUPE, it would be a matter of luck as to whether a change of branch had been recorded, whereas the AUEW would keep a record in both former and new branches, as well as at headquarters. Even if it was recorded, branches vary considerably, sometimes even within the same union, as to how long they will preserve such a record, the length depending to a large extent on the secretary's interest in such matters, and the amount of storage space available. The T&GWU has a permanent national record of change of branch, whereas each of the NALGO branches decides for itself what to record, and for how long.

Formal rules governing internal access to records of voluntary organisations are rare, with the result that disclosure of information depends on custom and practice, the personal attitudes of the record-keepers, and the ostensible purpose of the member seeking the information. In general, the lower the enquirer in the hierarchy, the less likely it is that he will be given the information. Often, even in the case of trade unions, records are kept at the home of the secretaries, though in some cases they have to be produced at branch meetings. Again, the question of internal access is transformed once the data have been computerised; code words would be necessary to log in, effectively preventing one branch from acquiring information about another, but allowing headquarters to see everything.

All the officials to whom I spoke were willing to help the police even if no warrant had been issued, despite the fact that all the interviews took place during the 1984–5 miners' strike. Their response would be different, however, if an alleged offence had taken place as a result of the union's own actions – for example, on a picket line. Several used such phrases as 'the public good' or 'doing as you would be done by' in order to express a general view that although the union was not there to police its own members, common sense dictated that the law of the land should not be hindered by a bureaucratic or ethical stance on confidentiality. In some cases they would be prepared to divulge an employer's name, rather than the home address, which might be outdated anyway. Unions also co-operate with the Race Relations

Board in the investigation of alleged discrimination by members (see Commission for Racial Equality, 1983). Most other enquirers would be treated on merit, and many unions would be suspicious that there might be a political organisation, a private investigator, or worse still, a journalist, behind the request for data about a member. Once bona fides have been established, however, and officials can be convinced that it is in the interest of the member concerned, help would probably be given to a wide range of bodies such as the DHSS, the Salvation Army, bank trust companies, or individual relatives to' establish contact with the members they are seeking.

Registers of certain professions have to be maintained by law: these are doctors, apothecaries, chiropodists, dieticians, medical laboratory technicians, occupation therapists, physiotherapists, radiographers, remedial gymnasts, dentists, veterinary surgeons, farriers (sic), pharmaceutical chemists, opticians, nurses, midwives, health visitors, and architects. The keeping of statutory registers in each case is designed to prevent anyone acting unqualified in such a capacity. Each has its own rules of content and accessibility, and of course there are many other professions for which registers of one kind or another are available. Space prevents a closer look at more than two of these – teachers and nurses.

Teachers

Teachers are free to choose whether to join one or more of the several trade unions for the profession, and have no professional body corresponding to, for example, the BMA for doctors. However, any who teach in schools in the public sector (or in private schools which have opted into the State superannuation scheme) should have Qualified Teacher Status accorded by the Department of Education and Science (DES) which holds records of those teachers in its Darlington office. The Main Mechanised Record of Teachers, started in 1962, shows current and historical data relating to each teacher's name, date of birth, National Insurance number, initial training qualifications, service, salary, elections, and anything relevant to the calculation of superannuation contributions and benefits. Teachers having QTS are given a DES number, which consists of two digits relating to the date of initial training, followed by others in a chronological distribution sequence.

No records have been removed from the computer since its

commencement; an additional manual file, including correspondence which is their best source for an up-to-date home address, is destroyed when a teacher-pensioner reaches the age of eighty five, or three years after the teacher's death (about which the DES is informed by personal representatives, employers, or by HM Paymaster-General's Office if the teacher has retired). Normally only the current employer (usually an LEA) is known to the Department, so that it is not uncommon for the DES temporarily to lose track of some teachers, especially when they are not currently employed, and occasionally have to use the services of the DHSS for forwarding mail (see pp. 94–9). Once in receipt of a pension, however, the address can be traced through the records of HM Paymaster-General's Office.

Persons who have been determined (following court proceedings) to be partially or totally unsuitable for employment as a teacher are placed on List 99, in various categories – not to be employed in a girls' school, for example. List 99 is circulated on a confidential basis to employers, schools and training establishments to ensure that they do not appoint proscribed persons. The list, which contains name, date of birth and DES number, is updated at six-monthly intervals. In certain circumstances it is open to teachers to apply for reinstatement following a period of exclusion and the names of fully reinstated persons are then removed from the list. In addition names are removed when an individual is known to have died or has reached the age of eighty. In connection with List 99, the DES is notified by the police, through the Home Office, whenever a teacher is brought to court, or by LEAs for other forms of misconduct. If, however, the court appearance was before he or she became a teacher, it is possible that the DES will not have been informed, especially before 1981 when the regulations were tightened.

The DES is willing to forward letters to teachers, if necessary through the last-known employer, and frequently does so, unless it is believed that the enquiry is not in the teacher's interest. The Department will co-operate with the police even when provision of information would not be in the teacher's interest. The records are kept in sequence of DES number, but this can be identified if you can provide instead the date of birth or last employer with the teacher's name. It also may help if you can provide the maiden name in the case of women teachers who have married.

Nurses

Following the Nurses, Midwives and Health Visitors Act of 1979, a unified register has been created for those professions by the United Kingdom Central Council (UKCC), which replaces the several separate registers which formally existed for those professions in the different nations within the UK. All those registered have been allocated a Personal Identification Number (PIN), consisting of two letters denoting year of training or of entering the profession and six characters which are partly a unique entrant number and partly a code for the nation concerned. The system can be accessed by name also, and by the number formerly held before the creation of the PIN in 1984.

Unusually, and to its credit, the UKCC has taken the trouble to issue a leaflet which is available to all when they register, explaining the meaning of the PIN system and the contents of the register. There are about one and a quarter million entries to the register, though only between 500,000 – 600,000 nurses, midwives and health visitors are believed to be currently practising. It is also estimated that about 90,000 of the persons whose names are entered on the register are probably dead. In addition, there are about 100,000 students in training. There are plans to refine the register to show those who are practising or who wish to retain the right to practise. This Single Professional Register and Index of Training (SPRINT) contains in addition to the PIN and former numbers full name, and changes thereto, address, place of training, qualifications, place and date of birth and nationality. Any address (place of work, for example) can be used and although nurses, midwives and health visitors have a responsibility to advise the UKCC of any changes in their personal details, there appears to be no penalty for failure to comply except possible inconvenience. The United Kingdom Central Council is planning to change the registration fee system and to require all nurses, midwives and health visitors to pay a periodic registration fee. This new arrangement will be introduced in 1987. In preparation for this and also to ensure that the personal details held on the register are as up-to-date as possible the Council embarked on 'Operation Update' in 1985. During 1985 and 1986 every nurse, midwife and health visitor in the UK will be contacted and asked to fill in a form updating their personal details. SPRINT is computerised and accessed from the UKCC Headquarters at 23 Portland Place, London W1N 3AF, and the four National Boards have on-line access also, but to the training records part of the register only.

The UKCC will answer queries from the general public if confirmation of registration of an individual is needed – data will be confirmed but not offered. The UKCC is also willing to pass on sealed letters for relatives, for the Salvation Army, and where it is clearly in the interest of the nurse to receive it – from a bank trust company, for example. If the request is very urgent the nurse could be contacted directly by telephone or via her local police station. Outside the UKCC itself the police might be given personal information but only if a senior member of the Council's staff is satisfied that this is necessary, either through the production of a warrant or if that officer is satisfied that a warrant would be obtained. It is felt that this is consonant with the fact that SPRINT is maintained for the protection of the public and the policy is certainly in line with that of most public and private record holders to be found in Section C of this book.

C12—National Insurance

Contribution records of National Insurance (NI) provide the most widely used channel of communication between individuals of all unpublished government sources, not only by other government departments, but also by private individuals. The reason is clear: although the files cover probably as many individuals as those of the NHS or Inland Revenue, the DHSS provides a staff at the records complex at Longbenton, Newcastle upon Tyne, which answers queries from other government departments, and will forward mail for most private enquirers to identifiable individuals whose whereabouts are known. It must be stressed, however, that the DHSS is in no sense a missing persons bureau, and they will not help those who wish to be informed of an individual's address. NI records cover the whole of the UK, and it seems probable that within ten years the indexes will be linked with those of child benefit and retirement pensions (q.v.).

The content of the basic NI file has been described by Rule (1973). Each contributor has a card showing full name, sex, NI number, sequence of addresses (with dates of change), date of birth, date of entry into the record system, marital status, name and NI number of spouse, record of contributions paid and benefits claimed, and annotations (including periods of time spent abroad, in prison, or in psychiatric hospital). Records of supplementary benefit payments are still kept only in local DHSS offices.

The main changes since Rule's book appeared are not so much in content as in the consequences of earnings-related contributions, and of computerisation introduced about ten years ago. In brief, employers must now provide names, NI numbers and details of contributions of all employees to the Inland Revenue, whence the data is sent to DHSS Central Records. Self-employed and voluntary contributions are still flat-rate, however, and those people who have not decided to pay by direct debit still have stamp cards. The self-employed also pay an earnings-related contribution which is collected by the Inland Revenue with Schedule D income tax, but this is not recorded by the DHSS as it does not count for benefits. It is not clear what effect the abolition of the State earnings-related pension scheme would have. The operational inadequacies of this system for the identification of individuals result from the abandoning of the old NI card which employers (or the Department of Employment in the case of those unemployed) used to hold and forward annually to Central Records. Employers now have to collect only the name and NI number, and are not even compelled to send home addresses to the Inland Revenue. This system is strained by so many individuals and firms providing much inadequate information – some six million returns from the Inland Revenue have to be queried each year, at considerable cost to the DHSS. It was for this reason that the small plastic card showing the individual's NI number was introduced a couple of years ago, but was (in my opinion) poorly explained to the general public. This is now issued mainly to new registrants.

The NI number, while not always necessary for identifying individuals, is a very helpful key to doing so. It always consists of two letters, six digits, and a final letter, and is thus far more easily computerised than the NHS number (see pp. 53–5). With very few exceptions, however, they do not encode the same amount of information, being allocated on an almost random basis. The first two letters are only for convenience (letters giving far more combinations than digits, given the same number of characters), though a small number of identifiable letter combinations were used for direct transfer from Approved Society and pension schemes in 1948. The six digits are also issued sequentially and at random, though the Records Branch has 100 divisions each containing the records of all persons whose NI number ends with the same two digits. Thus two adjoining cards in the file will have only that in common, being different in surname, age, and geographical area. The final letter is, since 1975, vestigial, being a trigger for a particular quarter-year (A, B, C or D) when the old card expired and had to be exchanged before it was sent to Newcastle for the contributions to be checked and recorded. From 1948 until 1975, local social security offices were given blocks of numbers for sequential issue. For young people numbers were generally issued by careers offices; since 1975, there has been a sequential allocation of numbers by the computers at Newcastle. This allocation is now triggered as mothers receive new child-benefit books once their children are over fifteen years two months old, and notify the DHSS of their educational intentions. Anyone not identified by this procedure would eventually have to go to a local DHSS office, when a number will be allocated. A check will ensure that one has not already been issued to that person; there are no distinguishing features to the 'late entrants'' numbers.

There are, therefore, important differences between NHS and NI numbers. The first lasts for the whole of one's life, is of geographical and chronological significance, and (for anyone born since 29 September 1939) may be legitimately obtained by any other person. The NI number, however, is allocated only at sixteen plus, has no other significance than that of distinguishing between individuals, and an individual's employer would be the only source of information at all likely to divulge it, outside the family.

The computerised records survive the individual's progressing to a retirement pension; contribution records are removed from the computer but kept on microfilm; and the manual card is also kept indefinitely. They are stored in alphabetical order back to 1948. (A few pre-date this.)

The DHSS local offices may discover and record emigration (see pp. 154–5). Anyone re-entering the country after emigration should retain the original NI number, but (as noted on p. 154) there is no obligation on the part of the emigrant to register his departure with any UK government department. The system will be informed about those in psychiatric hospitals and those in prison, data which has been very occasionally misused (see the *Guardian*, 23 February 1984). Information about change of name, marriage or divorce depends on the good sense of the individuals concerned to provide it; the same applies to adoption (see p. 64). An alternative route for some of this information is through the records of the Inland Revenue. A permanent note will be placed on the record, if the Department is informed that the individual has died.

Computerisation of contributions data has led to a reduction of over 50 per cent in Central Records staff since James Rule's description of the Longbenton site, and clerks previously engaged in the manual recording of straightforward cases are now involved only with those which are too few, or too complicated, to be viable for computer programming. Among them is Special Section 'A', a group of about ten people, part of whose function is to forward letters, currently at the rate of about 800 per week. They perform this service for almost any who make the request, require no reason for doing so, and expect the letter for forwarding to be already sealed. Accompanying this sealed envelope, there should be the full name of the missing person, the date of birth (or approximate age if not known), the last-known address *which must be since 1946*, and the last-known marital status. Being able to provide the NI number (or Child Benefit/Retirement Pension Number if appropriate) is not essential, but considerably facilitates the identification of the individual being sought. Mail will *not* be forwarded, however, in certain circumstances: in known adoption cases; to battered wives; or generally where it is known that the letter will not be well received.

The work of Special Section 'A' all too frequently leads to the likelihood that the missing person has died. In such cases the sealed envelope is returned to the sender with a standard form indicating the possibility of death, and a reference to the date when and place in which the death grant was claimed; this will probably be sufficient to enable the enquirer to apply for a death certificate (see pp. 157–8).

The DHSS appears to be alone among government departments in providing a special staff unit to facilitate a mail-forwarding service. Anyone making such enquiries at other departments, e.g. at St Catherine's House, are referred to Special Section 'A', and it is one of the first routes by which agencies such as the Salvation Army or broadcasting programme researchers attempt to get in touch with individuals. Organisations wishing to get in touch with large numbers of individuals may also apply, and the Department will decide whether to support individual proposals, and the level of fee to be charged, in the light of the benefit to be derived by the public. So far, such research has been medical rather than sociological.

Such is the size of the Central Office at Newcastle that it might be thought an infallible means by which one person could get in touch with another in this country. Alas, this is far from the truth. Some estimates of success may be obtained from medical research projects which need to contact large numbers of individuals. Newhouse and Williams attempted to contact 4,811 male former employees of an asbestos factory and were successful in only about three-quarters of cases; they located only two-fifths of female former employees (*British Journal of Preventive and Social Medicine*, 21, 1, 1967). The system clearly found it difficult to maintain contact with women at the time of marriage; and both sexes slip through the net through change of name, emigration, or death. It is probable that local DHSS offices have more up-to-date addresses than Central Records, but Special Section 'A' does not consult them over these enquiries.

As the DHSS is a department of central government, its staff are subject to Section 2 of the Official Secrets Act (1911), though no charges have been brought against them. The internal penalty for deliberate divulging of information without authorisation would be dismissal; for unintentional divulging, it would be removal from access to sensitive data, demotion, and/or loss of pay. A parliamentary question to which successive Secretaries of State have been subjected *ad nauseam* concerns legitimate authorisation for disclosure, ever since Sir Keith Joseph defined what access was permitted to his department's records for tracing missing persons:

> Access to departmental records is limited to my officials. If the address of a missing person under 18 is known it will be given on request, to the police or the parents. In the case of a missing adult, my department is prepared to forward a letter, if an address is known, and to give assistance to the police if they are investigating a crime which is other than trivial. In maintenance and affiliation cases a missing man's address will, on request, be disclosed direct to the appropriate court. (*Hansard*, 6 April 1973)

Among the extraordinarily voluminous instructions for DHSS officials is the Department's counterpart of the Home Office's instructions to the police relating to the extent of the help which can be provided in cases of serious crime (normally given orally and in confidence) and of missing persons under the age of eighteen (see p. 24). There is no provision for divulging the address of an adult reported missing, yet it must often lie in the Department's power to do so. It would appear that there is, *prima facie*, a simple device which would reduce the burden on the police relating to the tracing of long-term missing adults while preserving the civil liberties of the individuals concerned, and that is for the Department to supply the police on request with a simple statement if it is known that the individual is alive, since being reported missing, so that the police can be assured (and can in turn assure the relatives) that foul play or accident need no longer be feared. As indicated in Section B1, the number of such requests concerning long-term missing adults would not be great.

Personal data from all records held by the Newcastle Central Office are legitimately divulged by the DHSS to a large number of other agencies. The Department of Employment, with over eight million enquiries per annum, has some terminal access to the index of fifty three million NI contributors, which includes name, address, sex and date of birth. Statistics relating to the number of requests from the police relating to serious crime are not maintained; nor are those of certain other types of request – data on industrial diseases to health and safety authorities, for example. The other receivers of large amounts of data from the DHSS are the Inland Revenue (over seventeen million enquiries per annum), and employers and occupational pension schemes (over one million); personal data is also given to other government departments – Customs & Excise, the Home Office, the Foreign Office, the Ministry of Defence, the Post Office, the Exchequer & Audit, and to the courts – and also, for a wide variety of reasons and amounts, to local authorities, fire departments, the NCB, social security authorities in other countries, hospital management committees, banks, building societies, and even schools. (For further details, see House of Commons Deposited Paper No. 543, 5 April 1984.)

The size and complexity of this record system and communications network makes it vulnerable to illegitimate penetration by outside interests. Most private detectives given the chance of access to any files normally closed to them would choose the DHSS records. In common with most other keepers of voluminous records, the DHSS is frequently approached by 'firms' who, when contacted on the normal 'phone-back' system, disclaim all knowledge of the enquiry, and only constant vigilance in verifying the telephone numbers given prevents the steady leakage of confidential data.

C13—The Inland Revenue

Outside the DHSS and GRO, Inland Revenue offices collectively contain the largest series of registers concerning live individuals in the UK, covering the majority of adults. Its two main functions (tax assessment and tax collection) are separately organised, though obviously related, the former still being on a district basis with manual files and indexes, the latter organised through PAYE and Schedule D. Each PAYE taxpayer is given a code which relates to the amount of tax payable, and a reference number which identifies his place of employment rather than him/her as an individual. The National Insurance number is also used because of liaison with the DHSS (see pp. 94–9). Some 98 per cent of tax due on the PAYE system is actually received.

Inland Revenue records contain the detailed tax history of the individual through his recent earning life, (including the family, employment and investment detail all too familiar to those who have to complete their annual tax return) some files being 'weeded' after seven years, others after twenty; the obsolete papers are destroyed. Even more important from our point of view, changes of address, of employer, and in many cases change of name, can be found on the record. Any change of tax district involves transfer of the file, but an appropriate record is kept by the first office. The files are maintained for as long as administratively necessary, which in effect means little longer than the death of the individual, and are then destroyed. Only selected, departmental records are preserved permanently, many of which are transferred to the Public Record Office, and are subject to a thirty-year statutory closure rule. The only tax files of individuals which are open to the public are those of defaulters from the period of the Napoleonic wars.

Following an experimental period in the West Midlands, computerisation of PAYE is scheduled for all districts, to be phased between 1985 and 1987. Beside the obvious implications for the numbers of staff involved and the implementation of the Data Protection Act, the development will facilitate a far more rapid introduction of governmental tax changes; it will also make for a more efficient exchange of information with the DHSS which has been necessary for National Insurance contributions since 1975.

Being part of the Civil Service, staff working for Inland Revenue are subject to the Official Secrets Acts, and in-house training has been efficient enough to ensure that no prosecution has needed to be brought. Even without the Acts, there is a penalty of dismissal or disciplinary action for any official who deliberately divulges information without proper authority, and this would include a taxpayer's address. Outside the strictly controlled exchange with the DHSS, statutory information given to the Board of Customs & Excise, and very limited help given to the police in investigating only the most serious crimes (including drug trafficking in the near future), there is minimal co-operation with other government agencies, a characteristic shared with Customs & Excise (see Young (1978)). Neither the Treasury nor the Chancellor of the Exchequer himself have access to individual tax files (Franks Report; Flaherty (1979)). The Inland Revenue's rights of search are great enough to cause their officials relatively few problems of accessibility to the files of other departments, local authorities, employers, banks and many other institutions whose records are described in this book.

The information contained in Inland Revenue files has proved too alluring for some private detectives to resist. The Ace Detective Agency case in 1973 showed that this was one source of evidence illegally obtained, and the Younger Report highlighted a case in 1969 when two agents were each fined £5,000 for impersonating Inland Revenue officials in an effort to trace missing debtors. In their written evidence to the Franks Committee, the Board of the Inland Revenue proposed the use of the Official Secrets Act against any tracing agent seeking to gain information from official sources.

As already noted, in March 1983 Greville Janner asked a series of questions in the Commons about the assistance given by various government departments to individuals and agencies who try to trace missing persons. One, addressed to the Chancellor of the Exchequer, asked 'whether Her Majesty's government will introduce legislation to require the Inland Revenue to forward or redirect mail from relatives of missing persons seeking to trace them while maintaining full confidentiality'. Nicholas Ridley gave a remarkably full reply. While indicating that the rules prevent Inland Revenue from disclosing the whereabouts of third parties,

it is already its practice to assist, where possible, by forwarding or redirecting mail from relatives who are seeking to trace missing persons. The Revenue's ability to help will depend crucially upon the accuracy of the information given to it and on whether it can match it with its own local records. It cannot, on grounds of administrative cost, provide an open-ended forwarding or redirecting service, but within reasonable bounds it does its best to assist. By passing on communications the Revenue does not accept any responsibility in the matter and will advise the addressee that his address has not been disclosed to the person who has asked it to forward the communication.

In view of this, I cannot accept that legislation would be either necessary or, indeed, desirable. (*Hansard*, 4 March 1983).

I suspect that, not for the first time, some tax officers may have been taken somewhat by surprise by this statement of policy by a minister in the House; certainly the Salvation Army had been advised that no such help could be forthcoming. However, because Mr Ridley's words were *ex cathedra*, tax officers were advised through their in-house journal, the *Revenue Record*, to refer enquiries on how the policy should operate to Personnel and Accommodation in Bush House.

Thus the Inland Revenue now forwards, or redirects, mail for people who are trying to contact missing *relatives*. Enquiries should be sent to the last-known tax district office of the missing person, enclosing a sealed letter to be forwarded, and an accompanying letter to the Inland Revenue providing the full name, the last-known private UK address, the tax reference number, if known, the name and address of the last known employer (with dates), and the reason for your request. If you do not know the relevant tax district, you should send the same two letters to the Management Division (Personnel), Section M1/5, NW Wing, Bush House, Aldwych, London WC2B 4PP.

C14—Marriage

Since 1 July 1837 a valid marriage in England and Wales has been in one sense a public event, for a representative of the State must be present when it takes place. Rules governing marriage are currently under review (see Efficiency Scrutiny Report, 1985). The representative may be a registrar of marriages at a register office ceremony, a clergyman or member of the congregation appointed as an 'Authorised Person' in the case of many church services, or a registrar of marriages in a church which has not been granted this 'AP' status.

The information recorded has remained unaltered, whatever the form of ceremony, for almost 150 years: the registration district and place of marriage; the names, ages, marital status, occupation, residence, signatures, and the fathers' names and occupations, for both bride and groom. The signatures of the witnesses are also entered, with the name of the officiating registrar or minister; and finally, how the marriage has been arranged (see below).

Many churches keep copies of their ceremonies, and these are accessible through the goodwill of the minister and also (in the case of the Church of England only) the payment of any fee which he may charge. Anyone may buy a copy of anyone else's marriage entry, the fee being £5. The Superintendent Registrar of Marriages also keeps a copy of all marriages in his area, and compiles a series of indexes incorporating the names of both bride and groom. Access to the *index* is free for any single, specified event, but there may be a long search in some districts because each church is indexed separately. Access to the registers themselves (except for those currently being compiled) is forbidden by the Registrar-General.

The General Register Office at St Catherine's House, 10 Kingsway, London, also receives a copy, and a national index for England and Wales is compiled, showing bride and groom, each cross-referenced. Access to the registers is again forbidden; a copy of any marriage entry may be bought for £5 (£10 by post). Anyone may buy a copy of anyone else's marriage entry.

Marriages in the Anglican Church may be arranged by banns or (very rarely nowadays) by episcopal licence. Almost all other marriages must be announced for three weeks in advance by a Notice in the Register Office(s) of the district(s) where the bride and groom live. Notices are kept for at least five years. Aliases, or 'formerly known as' information should be displayed, and should subsequently appear on the marriage entry.

C15—Electoral registers

Lists of all persons entitled to vote at general elections have been published annually since 1832, and the statutory duty to prepare those registers falls on the 403 Electoral Registration Officers (EROs) in England and Wales in the employment of each local authority. Their actions are prescribed by instructions from several quarters – the 1983 Representation of the People Act and its associated Regulations (contained in Statutory Instrument No 435) and an advisory Code of

Practice (1984) issued by the Home Office. Local government finance also influences the effectiveness with which they carry out the necessary data collection.

The register itself is published annually on 15 February, and takes effect the following day for twelve months. It shows the name and address of each elector, together with the date of birth of persons ('attainers') who will reach their eighteenth birthday during those twelve months and who will therefore be eligible to vote on or after that date. Because the register is also used for local government elections, it is normally arranged by wards, then polling districts, and by alphabetical order of streets within each. In some rural areas, however, this arrangement is impractical, and the electors are presented in alphabetical order of surname. Anyone having the right to vote in both local and European elections but not in general elections is distinguished in the published register, but those over the age of sixty-five are marked only on copies held by the ERO and the Crown Court. This last information is used in order to identify those exempted by age from jury service. I know of no ERO who checks the accuracy of this return; some people who are over the age of sixty-five will not declare themselves to be so; equally, it seems an easy way to avoid jury service for anyone prepared to risk the penalty of £100 for giving false information.

In the 1970s, the Government considered increasing the information collected by the electoral registration system by adding, for example, age, sex, marital status, and address twelve months earlier, and the issue will probably re-emerge if rates are to be replaced by a poll-tax which has been incorrectly associated during recent debates with electoral matters; indeed, having a poll-tax record would call into question the need for an electoral register in the first place. Eventually, it was decided to abandon such a scheme because it was felt to threaten the main purpose of the register, through reactive disruption.

Studies of this system by the OPCS in 1982 revealed wide discrepancies between local authorities, and serious (and worsening) deficiencies in the registers themselves. As a result, the Home Office held a series of consultative meetings with EROs in order to rationalise and improve the system. As the electoral register is one of the two most commonly used sources for tracing missing adults, it is important to understand the causes of these difficulties.

For the register commencing 16 February, the base date for

collection of names and addresses is the previous 10 October, and all householders are required to complete Form A with the relevant data. If Form A is not returned, however, despite reminders and/or personal visits by canvassers, the ERO must in practice take one of four courses of action: (a) establish the presence of an elector by further investigation using what Statute directs are 'reasonable steps to obtain information'; this might involve questioning neighbours, or reference to local authority sources such as rents and rates; (b) repeat names included at that address in the previous register; (c) delete the earlier names from the new register; (d) prosecute those failing to return Form A. Clearly there are disadvantages with each of these. The first can leave the ERO open to the accusation of political bias according to which methods he uses, or of prying into personal affairs – some refuse to complete Form A because it would be a public acknowledgement that they are living together unmarried. The second is by far the commonest course of action, but it results in many names of deceased persons, or those who have removed, (amounting to between six and nine per cent of total) being on the register which, in turn, opens the possibilities of personation at elections. The third can disfranchise large numbers of people (about six per cent). The fourth runs counter to all the best intentions of local government, and is again not consonant with the low profile which most EROs believe is desirable for the smooth operation of the system. At least in this last case, however, the ERO could scarcely be accused of political bias, and the Home Office now seems to be encouraging greater use of the threat of prosecution, following improved data collection methods, in order to improve the accuracy of the registers. The cost of prosecution might outweigh its benefits, however. Perhaps the penalty for giving inaccurate information or non-completion of the form should always be included in Form A itself.

It will be noted that, for the purposes of tracing missing persons, the second and third of the above courses of action lead to serious problems. According to the policy of an individual ERO, names might appear there on the register. Normally, EROs are not informed of the equally; people are sometimes living at an address though they do not appear there on the register. Normally, EROS are not informed of the deaths of residents in their area, so a deceased person may be sent not only Form A but also voting cards, sometimes to the distress of relatives. Yet the District Medical Officers have this information supplied every month by the GRO, and could make it available. This would not only reduce the embarrassment and improve the accuracy of the register; it would also reduce the potential for double voting. The advent of a poll-tax, or 'community/residents charge' system of financing local government will clearly have to be far more accurate and efficient, and could have a significant effect on the government's ability to keep track of individuals.

The 1982 surveys showed that certain categories of elector fared particularly badly from the present system, especially servicemen's wives, young voters, the unemployed, ethnic minorities, and people in privately rented accommodation; London and Wales had the most incomplete registers.

Between 28 November and 16 December, the ERO must display a draft of the new register (or a list of new and deleted voters) in a public place – usually post offices, council offices, and public libraries, though Todd & Dodd (1982) found that some EROs displayed them also in Citizens Advice Bureaux, shops, churches, church halls, parish offices, and police stations. Public awareness of this facility should be increased as a result of better publicity; in the past, amendments resulting from this public view of the draft have been very few, especially in large populations.

Since 1980, it has been possible to add names after the publication of the new register, though not between the calling of an election and the election date. The calling of a general election towards the end of a five year term does have a significant influence on the completeness of the register – electors are more likely to ensure that their names are included, and local authorities are more willing to spend money on the personal canvassing of addresses. The law does not allow for a name to be deleted once the register has been published, however.

A copy of the register is issued free to the Secretary of State at the Home Office, the Registrar-General, the British Library, the Crown Court, and to election candidates. Local libraries and record offices will also retain a copy. Certain official bodies can purchase the register at reduced rates, though the Inland Revenue does not seem to have the need to do so, and the police sometimes have access to the local authority's computer on which it is stored. Anyone can buy a copy of the register for any area, if there are spare copies available, at a current cost of £1·50 for every 1,000 names or part thereof. Among those normally in this market are political parties, credit agencies (see pp. 37–8), insurance companies and churches; record companies and hotels also buy the register because they can discover from it the names, addresses and dates of birth of attainers, as potential customers.

Amending an already published register is easy for those EROs who have access to computing or word-processing facilities, some eighty-six per cent in 1982. Only the former, however, is useful for indexing the register, or reproducing it in alphabetical order, the so-called 'alpha listing'. This exercise has no basis in statute or government regulations, and is undertaken for, and at the expense of, the local authority. If the ERO uses the council's main computer, it might be another department in the authority which runs it off, and the ERO is sometimes unaware that it is being done. (Having been assured by one ERO that he possessed the only copy, and that he destroyed it each time a new one was produced, I was told by the public library across the road that they processed copies going back several years.) I have no estimate of the number of areas which have the electoral register in alphabetical order of surname, but it is clearly a very important source in the search for 'lost contact' friends and relations.

It is also interesting from the point of view of gaining some insight into attitudes of local government officials towards confidentiality of data. When an ERO produces a street-by-street register, he is fulfilling his duty under statute and Home Office regulations. The alpha listing is produced additionally for the council's own purposes and, it is argued, is thus presenting the data in a way the electors themselves might not approve of. Furthermore, there is every lilelihood that the alpha listing would be used for purposes other than voting – for example, by debt collectors, or less savoury characters.

The counter arguments are, in my view, much stronger. The larger of the debt collection agencies and credit data firms (to which private detectives can have legitimate access) already buy copies of the normal register, and thus have the alpha listings, with annual amendments, available via their own computer. The local authority is therefore denying the general public access to the lists produced with ratepayers' money to which outside bodies *can buy* access. Most private detectives can also gain information surreptitiously from the local authority's own copy – and anyway, I am never sure why some officials seem bent on hindering the work of debt recovery when they are not owed the money themselves. Names and addresses for eighty per cent of households can already be seen in alphabetical order in the telephone book and there are directories, such as Kelly's, which may list householders alphabetically, as well as topographically or by trade. The information requested on Form A is not declared to be confidential, and the data itself is published (with the exception of the identification of the over-65s); indeed, in some rural areas, it is already published in alphabetical order, as all areas were by law in the nineteenth century. The alpha listing is certainly a more convenient form of checking the presence and accuracy of one's own entry, as well as for the many non-electoral uses to which it is *already* put – for issuing library cards, for example, or for checking charge accounts or applications for television hire.

The result of diverging views among ERO's is a wide disparity in practice among those which do produce an alpha listing, and even councils with apparently similar political views can have radically different policies on the matter; Manchester, for example, does not allow its public library or even the police to have a copy, but Southwark allows free public access through its library service. Nor are the libraries themselves free from this diversity of approach, though in my view when they withhold the document from public access, they are showing an uncharacteristic degree of secrecy and paternalism by ascribing underhand motives to the general public.

Replies to a letter in the *Local Studies Librarian*, 3, 2 (Winter, 1984) indicated a wide variety in practices by librarians. Many did not even know that the alpha listing existed in their area, but have now managed to secure a copy for the library. Others knew it existed, but were not allowed a copy. Some had been given a copy, but only on condition that the public could not have access to it – though they could answer enquiries by using it. Other libraries were allowed to give access, but chose not to do so – some claimed, incorrectly, that the ERO *had* forbidden public access; others, that the library was short of space; and one, having allowed access in the past, has now (quite irrationally) closed it for thirty years because of the Data Protection Act.

Both EROs and librarians are regularly approached for help in tracing individuals via the register, especially by those for whom distance makes a personal visit difficult. In these circumstances, both types of official are normally pleased to assist, and the alpha listing is then, of course, particularly useful. If a business is making the enquiry, there might be a small charge. A stamped, addressed envelope should be enclosed with the request for information. If, however, the motives of the enquirer are in doubt, EROs in particular are less inclined to help, possibly fearing involvement in civil action or domestic strife – yet all they are doing is to facilitate public access to information which is already available to them.

C16—The census

There is already a considerable literature on the subject of the decennial British censuses which have been taken in every year ending with 1 since 1801 (except 1941). From their cautious beginnings as little more than a head count, censuses have become increasingly more complex, the questions in 1981 including domestic circumstances (rooms, tenure, amenities); transport; marital status; usual address; country of birth (place of birth ceased to be asked in 1961); nature, address, and mode of travel to place of employment; qualifications; and the signature of the head of household must be supplied. The 1939 enumeration of England, Wales and Scotland led to the compilation of the National Register, and was used as the basis for wartime identification and rationing; in 1952, it was taken over as the basis for the NHS Central Register (see pp. 50–8). The 1939 National Register recorded Identity Number, name, address, sex, marital status, occupation and, for the only time in any such enumeration, date of birth. The Armed Services were enumerated only if they were on leave on the relevant date (29/30 September). For the questions asked in each census since 1801, see Lawton, 1978.

The White Paper on Security of the Census of the Population (1973) found only the tiniest scraps of evidence that the hundred-year confidentiality rule had been broken, and until 1971 there had never been a prosecution for this offence. Any breach would take place at the time of collection; thereafter, the enumeration forms are kept by the OPCS under stringent security conditions, and are accessed by their staff solely for the extraction of statistical data until the papers are eighty years old (when in some circumstances, individual entries of named persons may be quoted for a fee; see Rogers, 1985).

The modern census is inaccessible for information about individuals, not only to the general public, but also to any other government department and to most officials within the OPCS; there is no provision for access even by search warrant (see Bulmer (1979)). With that sort of security, I am quite happy to include answers about myself to questions which have not even been asked, let alone to those which have; it is my way of talking to my descendants, to whom they will be available in three generations' time. It might also be said that, even if the census *were* available, the task of finding any person in it is colossal without the sort of street index which is compiled before the hundred-year release date; the information also becomes rapidly outdated.

C17—Prison and Probation Service Records

Records of some 47,000 people in British prisons come under Section 2 of the 1911 Official Secrets Act, though those of probation do not. They are laid down in Home Office regulations, and are maintained by the prison concerned; they include name, address, details of offences and sentences, and other details necessary to facilitate family welfare, training and treatment, decisions of the Local Review Committee and Parole Board, decisions concerning granting of leave, and also a search in the event of an escape. Most are destroyed twenty years after the prisoner's discharge, though a few are forwarded to the Home Office for consideration as to whether they should be permanently preserved under the Public Records Acts – if so, they will remain closed to public access until they are 100 years old.

If you wish to write to someone in prison, but are unaware of which establishment he is in, you can write to the Prison Department of the Home Office, asking them to forward a letter on your behalf; alternatively, your local probation office may be able to arrange the same facility. By either route, the letter will probably be opened and, if necessary, censored, by the prison authorities before it reaches its destination, though recently, some prisons have been experimenting with flexible schemes of censorship involving sampling.

Outside Home Office, prison, probation and police access, only research workers may acquire data from these records. The subjects for investigation, and arrangements for confidentiality, must first be approved by the Home Office, and research workers are required to sign a declaration relating to the Official Secrets Acts; there has been a successful prosecution under Section 2 for an offence relating to the divulging of data from prison records.

On the whole, it is during the period following a spell in prison that individuals often lose contact with former acquaintances and even relatives. The local Probation Service deals with some clients in this situation, together with many others involved in, for example, matrimonial and adoption cases – see Jarvis (1980) for the full list of areas.

Nationally, they deal with one third of a million clients annually. There is no national list, and most files are still maintained on manual systems.

Probation records are very full (see Jarvis, 1980, for details), being in the general tradition of social work in this respect, and are laid down by legislation and the Probation Rules. They may include full name, date of birth, religion, address (with physical description thereof), names, ages, and other details of close relatives in the family, education, work history, medical history, use of leisure time, prison and criminal record (including CRO number), and what Jarvis calls 'the thinking part of the permanent record' – the casework assessment and progress notes. If a new offence is committed, a new probation file will be created, cross-referenced to the first. Despite Jarvis's description, the record is kept for a minimum of only five years from the date on which the subject ceased to be a client – the actual time in each authority will depend to a large extent on storage facilities. Furthermore, there are currently pilot schemes using a shorter form of the normal full records.

The probation office dealing with referred ex-prisoners will probably be that of the area in which they intend (or are required) to live. Again, if this is not known, a letter for forwarding can be left with any probation office, which might be able to locate the appropriate one if name and prison from which the prisoner had been discharged are known. In these circumstances, mail would not be opened. Probation officers are normally willing to consider the forwarding of mail of clients, but may require to know the reason for the request.

Legitimate access to the information in probation officers' files is described generally in the Probation Rules (1983) 22(3) – 'persons authorised by the probation committee or a probation inspector appointed by the Secretary of State but to no other persons'. In practice, this leaves some discretion in the hands of the officers; information from the files would be given to various other agencies where it was judged a relevant enquiry for specific purposes – for example, to the Social Services where there is a joint interest in a non-accidental injury case; to a doctor where there is a need for psychiatric assessment treatment; or to the police where the Probation Service has to notify them of a parolee's change of address. There appear to be no guidelines relating to the Salvation Army, but of course nothing would be divulged to a private detective or any member of the general public. In their case, if contact is deemed to be in the interest of the client, he will probably be asked to contact the enquirer direct.

C18—Health visitors' records

These records can provide a continuum on each child from before birth to adulthood. The heads of information which they contain are basically laid down by the DHSS, though each District Health Authority can supplement them with extra information. They contain a wealth of data relevant to the provision of sound professional advice to the mothers as clients, as well as to other health professionals. A series of record cards is compiled at successive stages, describing the development, and environment, of the child's health.

The DHA is notified of each birth by the District Medical Officer, a line of communication which goes back to the Notification of Births Act (1907). Health visitors normally record the name, address, date of birth, place in the family, and GP of each child; the name, date of birth, and medical history of both parents; the mother's antenatal and postnatal record; the medical condition of the child; vaccinations; the social circumstances of the family, including details of accommodation; results of child development screening tests; and an educational record, including schools attended, the results of regular, though occasional, health checks, and a record of illnesses. Space is provided to record changes of name and address. Following adoption, a new file will be created, the old one destroyed, and (by some DHAs), the new file marked 'Adopted'. The file will be transferred, if appropriate, from one DHA to another.

Well over half the DHAs have computerised child health records, and in these areas, each child will be allocated an identity number. This is a national scheme, though the number is allocated at regional level. The number has eighteen characters. Three provide a code for the district in which the child is currently residing; a letter and three numbers provide a Russell Soundex code for the surname (Smith being S530, for example); six digits give the date of birth; the next gives the sex; two suffixes allow children with the same surname, sex and date of birth to be distinguished from each other; and finally, there is a computer check digit on modulus 37. This number is not used in correspondence with the family concerned, and will be changed when the child moves to a new district, or is adopted, for example.

The main function of computerisation is to facilitate the call and recall of children for routine examinations such as vaccinations. If the family moves and cannot be found, the computer entry can then be 'flagged' in order to match the details with others for whom there is otherwise 'no trace'; often, however, the children who are lost to the system have gone abroad.

These records are maintained until the individual child reaches the age of twenty-five (though the computer system is only some fifteen years old). They are kept by the DHA, which normally maintains a base index of children in the area – thus, incidentially, knowing which children *should* be at school when the LEA does not know. The LEA would be told, however, if a specified child is on a school roll, from this index. Health visitors are also called upon to help adult clients, but the records in their case will probably be found in local hospital files. Access to data in health visitors' records has been the subject of one of the Körner reports and the DHSS discussion paper on access to health records generally; see pp. 143–6.

Potentially, this system should be useful for tracing families who move. If this is to a new DHA, a note will be retained, although the main file is passed forward. My impression is that DHAs could be approached to forward letters, via the new DHA, but are rarely if ever asked to do so. However, the ability of the system to keep permanent track of the whereabouts of children who move is less than perfect; there can be falsification of details by outside informants, and the DHA has to keep 'lost and found' files for those who transfer without formal notification. Information comes through GPs, as well as the health visitors themselves, but sometimes has to be supplemented by data from relatives, friends, and neighbours. The fact that the child care number can change, and is not even used by many areas, does not help this process.

Health visitors have their own missing persons in the shape of those suspected of being in contact with sexually-transmitted diseases; DHAs can nominate or appoint personnel to be involved in this 'contact tracing'. They use many of the locally available sources described in Section C, but work under the considerable difficulty of being unable to inform those able to help of the purpose of their enquiry.

C19—Child benefit

Child benefit (formerly family allowance) records for England, Wales and Scotland are maintained by the DHSS at the Child Benefit Centre at Washington, PO Box 1, Newcastle upon Tyne NE88 1AA. The Centre is informed of births when the parents claim a maternity grant and/or child benefit, both of which are processed by the same section. Thus the system need not necessarily include all live births in the country, but will include some files which resulted in stillbirths. There are about seven million payees, receiving benefit for nearly twelve million children. It may soon be replaced by 'family credit'.

The records themselves are centred not on the children but on the mothers, each of whom is given a number which normally remains with her, no matter how many children she has. (Rarely a new number will be issued if the mother fosters or adopts a child much later in life.) The numbers, after the letters CHB, consists of eight digits and are issued sequentially so have no intrinsic significance. Two further letters are provided as a computer check digit. On the allowance book, the number is followed by a serial number, which will differ for the same mother with each new allowance book, and relates to the actual orders contained within that book. An index to claimants and children separately is soon to be computerised.

The system records: the names of the claimant (and her alternate); their present and former addresses, and present and former post offices where collection has been arranged; the children in the family, with their dates of birth; the books issued, or record of payment by automatic credit transfer into a bank account; the National Insurance number of the claimant and/or her husband, though not in every case; and any alias used. Addresses are kept up-to-date via the Post Office. Obsolete data is removed from 'live' accounts after two years, and a computer file is retained until five years after the last payment has been issued.

Acheson (1967) noted that the system relies upon the honesty of the claimant for the recording of the death of a child, and the allowance order book instructs that the local social security office be informed of the event and the allowance book returned at that point; news of the death would also be picked up while the death grant exists, but the Government has declared its intention to abolish this, except for those claiming under a social fund. A back-up to the normal notification could be provided if the Registrar-General included the relatively few child deaths with the data which he regularly sends on deaths of the elderly (see p. 156).

DHSS officials can use these records, as they can use National Insurance records, for tracing persons; however, requests by the public for the forwarding of mail to missing persons should be sent to Special Section 'A' (see p. 97), not to Child Benefit. There is a long standing arrangement by which letters are forwarded on behalf of the Salvation Army in a few cases, but Child Benefit is not staffed to cope with an increased demand for this facility.

C20—Building society investment records

Building societies are developing at as fast a pace as any institution in this book, and the changes will, in my view, have significant implications for the data relating to investors which the societies currently record. They are, at present, relatively casual about addresses, and even identities, of their investors if only as a consequence of the system allowing no credit. It is of little concern to them *whose* money they are holding, so long as there are sufficiently accurate macro-statistics on which to base local and overall policies, and so long as they have fulfilled their obligations towards the Inland Revenue.

This is not to say, of course, that internal security is not tight; of those societies with total assets over £1,000 million (sixteen in all), only the National and Provincial has net yet erected security screens. Closed-circuit television, with video facility for recording, *inter alia*, all new customers, is now a commonplace feature of all branches.

Although interest on investment is taxed at source, this is at the standard rate. All managers are familiar with the investor who closes an account the day before the half-yearly statement, which would have been sent to a false address, or a proposed new account which has a totally false postcode.

However, all this will soon change when societies are allowed to give credit on an investment account – they would soon find themselves in financial trouble if their data collection were not considerably extended, and this is already happening to those opening cheque-book accounts. Following the lead of the banks, they too will introduce credit scoring systems. At the moment, it is normal to ask only for the name and correspondence address of investors, together with marital status (for women only), and directions concerning how the interest is to be paid. Only a minority (e.g. the BBBS and the Nationwide) request information about other accounts with the society though any with large computing facilities, such as the Halifax, will automatically cross-check new names and addresses with those on existing accounts. I know of none which asks about accounts with other societies. The Abbey National and the Nationwide are among the few which ask for occupation, and most require date of birth only from an investor under the age of eighteen (or under seven, in the case of the Alliance).

The other major change, from the point of view of this book, is the develpment of computer links. Between branches of the same society, of course, these are already commonplace, but extending them across different societies and into several agencies of the state (e.g. electricity boards, the Post Office, and the DHSS) has been discussed. Automated teller machines are planned to cross both banks and building societies by 1987 (see the *Guardian*, 9 February 1985). It is obvious that, if these two developments were to take place, such a system would be an extraordinarily efficient means of surveying the investors concerned. It should be said, however, that such co-operation is quite alien to current building society attitudes and practices.

The numbers of investors are very large, though not quite as great as the figures suggest *prima facie* because of the unknown number of duplicate accounts in some societies. With that proviso, building societies claim to have over thirty-five million investors, which would suggest that a substantial majority of adults in this country are included.

The data recorded about them, together with the signed application for membership, are held for as long as the account is open, and for several years thereafter, the period depending as much as anything on storage facilities. The Anglia preserves the record for a further twelve years, National & Provincial for ten, the Leicester for five, but the Woolwich indefinitely. When an application has been received the new account (*not* the investor) is given a reference number, the first element of which (probably consisting of three digits, as the largest societies, the Halifax and the Abbey National, have over 600 branches, though the proposed Nationwide/Woolwich merger would have had almost 1,000) will be a branch code; the next element a number allocated chronologically; and the last a computer check digit. The whole might be preceded by a letter or number denoting the type of account. Normally the account number will not change even if the account is transferred to another branch, but would be replaced if the passbook were stolen.

Change of address is recorded as and when the society is informed by the investor. Former address(es) are retained on file by most societies, even if only at branch *or* headquarters; if the record is maintained on a manual system an old record card might be discarded if there were many changes of address.

Like banks, building societies have their own 'missing persons' in the sense that they lose track of some investors whose accounts become dormant after a period of inactivity of perhaps two to five years (depending on the society involved). Again, most such accounts contain small amounts, so that little is done to locate the owner beyond sending a letter to the last known address. If the balance is substantial, the society's headquarters will normally assume responsibility for locating the owner, but in this they are severely hampered by their own rule of confidentiality which prevents them from explaining why they are trying to trace the individuals concerned!

This prevents them from being able to go through channels such as the NHS Central Register which would be able to help if assured that it was substantially in the financial interests of the individual concerned. Some societies transfer money from dormant accounts into a central 'unclaimed balances' fund, because having large numbers of such accounts lying idle in the normal system is an obvious temptation to internal fraud.

All branch managers approached for this survey would willingly pass forward unaddressed letters to their investors. Some might be curious as to the reason for the request, and may want it in writing. (Some managers expressed a preference that they contact the investor first, and ask him/her to get in touch with the enquirer.) Normally, there will be no stipulation as to whether the envelope should be open or sealed.

All this, however, begs the question of how it can be ascertained that an individual *is* an investor with a particular society. This knowledge might come from relatives or acquaintances, or from employers' records in the increasing number of cases where the salary is paid into a building society rather than into a bank (a relatively small number in most areas, perhaps one per cent in most, but up to ten per cent in a few). Banks themselves will have recorded whether a cheque has been paid into or out of a build society account (see pp. 75–6). However, if all else fails, it would be a matter of taking the enquiry to different societies until the enquirer strikes lucky. Although there are well over 200, it might not be such a long trek – over half the savers are with only four societies (the Halifax, Abbey National, Nationwide and Woolwich) and over ninety per cent are with one or other of the largest eleven.

Some managers (e.g. in the National & Provincial at the time of writing) would have to obtain an investor's address from head office if it was not known to him; in others, such as the Anglia, any branch official can obtain the address of an investor at another branch, though if only the name (not the number) was provided, information would be obtained for each person of that name. Societies vary considerably in the amount, and methods, of internal security which tries to ensure that such inter-branch enquiries are undertaken for bona fide reasons, and it is normal for all employees to sign an undertaking not to divulge information to those who have no right of access to it. I presume that building society employees, already having preferential mortgage terms from their employer, are the exception to the general rule that people entrusted with confidential information can be more easily bribed into releasing it shortly after a big increase in the mortgage rate.

Building societies exchange information with each other, with banks (though they do not provide the same status check service) and with private detectives whom they have hired. The Inland Revenue has the right of access to any account, and the facility for spot checks. The police with a warrant, or acting on the society's behalf, would be given information; if their enquiry was urgent and the matter serious enough, though no warrant had yet been issued, most managers would refer an enquiry to a higher authority within the organisation, though some might leave the information lying on the desk rather than pass it over officially. Additionally, access may be obtained by the society's agents, especially in those cases such as the Halifax which have installed terminals to the society's mainframe in some agents' offices.

Joint accounts which are in dispute are treated in exactly the same way as by banks; see p. 78. Until a dispute is signalled, either party can have any information about the account.

For teenagers running away from home, a building society offers more support than a bank account, which will not normally issue a cheque card until the account holder reaches the age of eighteen. A minor can open a building society account from which money cannot normally be drawn; however, the parent can sign a dispensation, no matter what the age of the child, allowing the society to issue withdrawals on the child's sole demand. If the account is in the child's name only, the parents would not be given access to information about it, in theory even if the child is missing from home and could be located through withdrawal data. See Mills (1976) for problems arising for societies with minors as members.

The Chief Registrar of Friendly Societies has determined, somewhat to the initial consternation of some building societies, that any candidate for a directorship should be given access to the names and addresses of all investing members so that election communications may be sent to them. Lest it be thought, however, that standing for the Board is an easy way to acquire this data on millions of individuals, conditions attaching to the nomination should be considered. A random survey of twenty societies shows considerable variation; but the candidate would be expected to have between £100 (Leamington Spa) and the normal £1,000 invested with the society; be under a certain age (e.g. sixty-six for Town and Country); have the nomination form signed by between three (Furness) and forty (Bristol & West) voting members who must have between £1 (Anglia) and an average of £1,250 (Bristol & West) invested. Furthermore, if any candidate fails to gain more than five to ten per cent of the total votes cast, he loses his deposit of between £0 (Bristol & West) and £250 (National & Provincial). No manager has been able to tell me how a candidate can make contact with potential signatories when membership of the societies is supposed to be confidential. Perhaps they have to canvas outside a branch office, hoping to find those with large enough investments. However, legislation following a Green Paper on the future of building societies may soon eliminate some of the larger variations between them.

Following an application in 1964, the Chief Registrar has also ruled that his power to allow a search of a register of members would be granted only in important and exceptional circumstances. From 1987, however, responsibility for supervising building societies will be transferred to a new Building Societies Commission; and shareholders in any building society which becomes a public company will, presumably, be tested for public scrutiny under the rules of the next Section (C21).

C21—Registers of shareholders

Sections 110, 111 and 124 of the Companies Act (1948, as modified by the Companies Act of 1967) lay down regulations concerning the compiling of registers of shareholders by all companies, showing at minimum their names, addresses, type and amount of holding, and date of acquisition. Firms with more than fifty shareholders must also prepare surname indexes, unless the register is already maintained in alphabetical order. In theory, these should be updated within a fortnight of each change. Only the most recent address will be shown, and with computerisation it is possible that firms will not retain earlier addresses anyway. Information about former shareholders should be kept for twenty years.

In practice, a notice of change of address sometimes reveals to the company that the full name had not been recorded in the first place (see London & Birmingham (1968)). It is also evident that, although it is in the interest of any shareholder wishing to receive correspondence, new issues, and dividends, to make sure that their current address is registered, by no means all do so. It should also be observed that not all shareholders buy directly, so often the address is that of a solicitor or bank.

Once every three years, a full list of shareholders, with the index, should be sent to the Registrar of Companies at Crown Way, Maindy, Cardiff, among the documents comprising each company's annual return; annual changes to the register are submitted in the interim. The Companies Registration Office holds these lists on microfiche until twenty years after a company's dissolution, the actual documents being stored for ten years.

On all but up to thirty working days in the year, companies must make their register of shareholders open to public inspection, for a fee of 5p, at their registered office, or at the office where the register is compiled. A copy of any section of the register may be bought, within ten days of the request, for a fee of 10p for each 100 words or part thereof. This is how, in the case of contentious takeovers such as that of Westland helicopters in 1986, shareholders can be approached directly by rival groups.

The Registrar of Companies has in the past experienced considerable difficulties in ensuring that firms make these annual returns; at the time of writing, an estimated thirty-three per cent are in arrears, though the majority are by only one year. The firms themselves clearly have the most up-to-date registers; addresses of all the registered offices of companies may be obtained from the 'List of registered offices' (known to librarians as the 'CRO directory'), issued by the Companies Registration Office.

C22—Estate agents

Ostensibly, it would appear that estate agents might be a very useful source of information for tracing persons who have changed owner-occupied properties. No single professional association regulates their activities, documentation or relationships, though the majority are members of the Royal Institute of Chartered Surveyors, the Incorporated Society of Valuers and Auctioneers, or the National Association of Estate Agents (Card (1979) suggested a seventy per cent membership; a more recent estimate suggests that some 2,000 firms, or fifteen per cent, are not members; see the *Guardian*, 16 April 1985.) The Estate Agents Act of 1979 does not subject them to the rules of confidentiality imposed on central and some local government bodies, falling short of a licensing system. Finally, even the larger firms do not normally issue the equivalent of the guidance manuals to be found on the shelves of bank or building society managers, though the Director-General of Fair Trading has general oversight of some of their work, in order to secure greater competence in performance and security for clients.

In reality, however, those wishing to trace the previous owner of a specified property may find that estate agents are of somewhat less help than this relative freedom from controls might suggest. There is no easy way to discover which agency, if indeed any, was responsible for arranging the sale, unless the subsequent owner or a neighbour can remember the transaction. Even then, double agencies are not uncommon, especially in the South of England, and at least one local council has attempted to ban agency boards from front gardens. The search might in the end necessitate a visit to the most likely firms culled from the Yellow Pages.

Estate agents normally maintain two sets of records. A full file on the sale of each property contains the names and addresses of the vendor and his solicitor, details of the property, names, addresses, and telephone numbers of all who express an interest in buying, and the name, solicitor, and building society of the eventual purchaser.

The files are indexed by vendor's surname, and by address. In the majority of cases, the new address of the vendor will not be recorded because correspondence will have been through his solicitor, through whom payment is normally made. It might be recorded, however, if the vendor has left the property well before the sale is complete, or if the estate agent dealing with his new property has consulted the firm in order to establish the client's ability to proceed with the purchase. Any firm which has had unfortunate dealings with solicitors might take steps to record future addresses of all vendors.

The length of time for which the above files are kept depends largely on the storage space available, and I have been quoted figures varying from four to twenty-five years. They are normally kept in the office which negotiated the sale.

Additionally, estate agents keep an abbreviated version of each, containing the name of the client, the address, and the transaction reference number in the main file series. Being little more than indexes, these may be kept infinitely, and I have seen some from well before the Second World War. They are used largely to study the effectiveness of the firm in acquiring clients in different parts of the district, and may, therefore, also be kept by the firm's head or regional office.

The files themselves are regarded as confidential, but may be easily accessed by anyone working in the relevant office or even the firm. A letter to a missing person would probably be forwarded on request, but only if the new address were known. The name of the vendor's solicitor, however, does not seem to be regarded as confidential, and would be given to almost any enquirer by the firms I consulted. An approach to the solicitor is much more likely to achieve the forwarding of the letter, but not the address itself. (Solicitors are bound by law to maintain confidentiality about a client's affairs, even when no longer instructed by him; disclosure without the client's permission could result in sanctions by the Law Society. What passes between a lawyer and client is the only professional relationship which cannot be exposed in a court of law; see Young (1978)). Far from being in cahoots with the estate agent, a solicitor will not divulge the client's new address even if he has moved leaving the fee unpaid. In those circumstances, an estate agent is likely to hire a private detective to locate the offender – possibly upon the recommendation of the same solicitor! Often, however, the estate agent will learn of the vendor's new address not from his own files, nor from the vendor's solicitor, but from the new occupant of the property concerned.

The police are given any information from most estate agents' files, and so normally are authorised enquirers from central or local government bodies (though one manager confessed to refusing the DHSS because of personal prejudice). Some would give a new address, if they had one for the client concerned, to the Salvation Army, or to any individual who seemed to have a good reason to request the information – for example, adopted persons seeking their natural parents, or a neighbouring shopkeeper trying to recover a bad debt. However, others would prefer to pass the buck and provide only the name of the client's solicitor. There is evident prejudice against private detecives (however good their clients' causes are claimed to be), and one manager professed that the only outsider to whom he would not give information would be a 'seedy, Mafia-type person' – but I did not press him on what he meant!

C23—Building society borrowers' records

Building societies have currently granted mortgages to about five million people, several times fewer than the number of investors. However, the amount of data collected and stored about each borrower is many times greater than that collected on investors; see pp. 115–16. This leads to a much greater certainty of identification and long term surveillance of the individuals concerned.

Most societies record the name, title, date of birth, current address, occupation, telephone number, other members of the household over the age of seventeen, income, name and address of employer (or accountant if self-employed), banker, how long with current employer, whether the applicant has been declared bankrupt or insolvent, whether he has an investment account with the society, whether he has taken out another mortgage, his solicitor, the name of the vendor and his agent, and the borrower's signature.

There are exceptions and additions to many of these main items: the Britannia records age, not date of birth; the Halifax does not record the vendor; the Middleton does not wish to know the accountant of a self-employed applicant; surprisingly, the BBBS does not record the banker; the National and Provincial will not ask how long the applicant has been with his current employer; and so on. On the other hand, the Alliance records former addresses within the previous two years; the Leicester want to know how long you have lived at your current address; and several societies record an employee's works number and marital status. All this information is, of course, as at the date of application, and much of it is rapidly outdated unless the borrower has cause to bring it up to date himself – if, for example, he becomes unemployed.

Each mortgage account (not borrower) is allocated a number, normally in two or three parts. There will be a number or letter to denote the type of account and the branch concerned; a second part is a number issued chronologically; and a third might be a computer check digit. If the account is transferred to another branch, many societies will issue a new number.

Borrowers' records are maintained both by individual branches and by head office, so that an employee in one branch does not always have the same ease of access to the account which he has with investment accounts. The account number would enable an enquiry to be made directly to the relevant branch; without the number, such an enquiry would have to be passed through the central records system at head office.

It is not normally in the interest of a borrower to close a mortgage account, and of course the file is maintained for as long as part of the debt remains unredeemed. However, once the debt has been paid off, the record is kept for a few years, the period depending on the demands on space, and how the data is stored. A manual system would be destroyed earlier than those on microfilm, but in practice most societies preserve them longer than the Woolwich (one year).

There is no straightforward way to discover which society has issued a mortgage to any one individual, but if it can be discovered where the 'lost contact' you are seeking had once lived or worked, there are several possible routes to the information – in the hope, of course, that he has remained with the same society at his new address as a borrower or an investor. Some methods (via an employer or bank) are referred to elsewhere; see p. 117. Additionally, the deeds of the house concerned will normally show which society was involved in any previous mortgage on it; those deeds may be held either by the present owner of the property, or by his own building society, and his permission would be required to obtain access to the information. (A branch manager or even employee might be able to acquire details from mortgage deeds held in another office of the same society, however.)

The present owner's permission would also be needed if the same details are sought from HM Land Registry. This is not open to the general public, though there is some pressure from the Law Commission that access should be widened. The registers of title may be inspected by the present owner or by anyone having a mortgage interest in it, by local authorities, or by court officials in relation to legal proceedings, though similar systems in other countries, including Scotland, are more open.

Access to building society borrowers' records by outside bodies is substantially the same as for investors' records; see p. 118.

C24—Local authority rates and rents

The rating system in England and Wales is, at the time of writing, once again under review by central government with a view to radical change or even abolition. Until that happens, a substantial part of local authority income comes from a system several hundred years old, based on an occupier's ability to pay. For most of that time, this ability has been crudely measured by a 'valuation' of buildings, an assessment undertaken nowadays by the Commissioners of the Inland Revenue. Those too poor to pay have always been exempted, and can apply for a rate rebate.

Most occupiers should pay rates – all owner-occupiers, and those with an exclusive tenancy which involves the occupier paying rent and rates separately. Where an inclusive tenancy is involved, however, the local authority will not necessarily record the names of tenants of a private landlord, and will have no connection with them unless the landlord defaulted. It is this group which will be potentially the greatest problem if rates were replaced by a poll-tax, for they may easily avoid inclusion on the electoral register, and probably use a pay-phone – they are thus difficult for a member of the general public to trace, unless they happen to be shareholders (see p. 120), for they are unlikely to appear in a Kelly's directory either.

Rates records have to be kept for a minimum of ten years after the ratepayer leaves the premises, but as most authorities now transfer the computer entry onto microfiche, former storage problems can be largely overcome, and the record kept much longer. There is a tradition of preserving rates books (the books as such have not been required since 1960), and many still exist from earlier centuries. Until computerisation, they were kept in sequence of address, though nowadays individual names can be accessed just as easily. As with rents, each address and sub-tenancy is given a reference, so the resulting rate number is very similar in construction to those of the public utilities, having area and street codes first, followed by the house number, sub-tenancies, changes within the financial year, and a computer check digit. A widow staying on at the same address as her ratepaying deceased husband will be given a new number, as she will be regarded as a new occupier.

More information will be held about those paying rent on local authority property. Once again, the basic record will relate to individual addresses and the name and address of the person responsible for paying rates on a specified property will normally be provided to any enquirer. Additionally, however, cards on occupiers will show former addresses and forwarding addresses; names and date of birth will be held for members of households claiming housing benefit, which links the local authority system to that of the DHSS. A register of defaulters will be maintained, from which names are deleted after death, or after unsuccessful attempts to locate those who abscond.

Most people are much more interested in taking steps to avoid being overcharged than in avoiding payment altogether. Application forms for the local authority to open and close accounts on specific dates are therefore in the records, and include both former and future addresses. This, together with address and financial statement, will normally be the sum total of the record; reference to the ratepayer's and rent payer's bank, of course, may also be included.

Most authorities are willing to forward unaddressed mail to former payers of rates and rents whose new addresses are known to them. However, in these days of local government retrenchment, I came across one which makes a charge of £5 for such a service if the enquirer is, for example, a solicitor or a building society. Even in their case, however, officers have the right to waive the fee if the purpose is basically humanitarian – for example, an enquiry from a relative or from the Salvation Army. Haringey refused this service even to the police in one reported case, however (see the *Guardian*, 8 January 1986).

In most areas, there appear to be no formal rules governing the divulging or exchange of information with other authorities, and practices do vary. As a gross generalisation, it is probable that they would give information to the police and to other local authorities, as well as to other departments within the same authority. There is also a mutual interest in sharing data with British Telecom, the DHSS, and the gas and water boards, though the electricity boards probably prove the most fruitful. With all such agencies, it commonly happens that an absconder is in debt to more than one, so mutual aid is in their interests. The variation in practice is because this exchange of information is often at a personal, unofficial, non-attributable level. Neighbours usually provide a useful source of information also.

As a result of such co-operation, local authorities know the whereabouts of approximately ninety five per cent of all defaulters and some feel that those still missing are not worth an intense effort to locate; others, however, will employ a private detective agency if their own inspectors fail to find the offender, but will probably spend only a few pounds on each case. See p. 37.

C25—The public utilities – electricity, gas and water board records

These records are arranged around addresses rather than individuals, and only the account holder – i.e. the person who signed the application for connection in the case of electricity and gas, the head of the household in the case of water – will be listed in them. Each address is given a reference number of about thirteen characters which will be found on the quarterly bill. This number will be arranged in coded form and will normally consist of (in sequence and with minor variations) a two-digit billing area, a five-digit street code, the number of the house in the street (uncoded), a sub-address number, an 'occupational cyclic digit' (indicating the number of different occupiers in that year or since the computer was installed), and probably a computer check digit.

The records are computerised, and do not come under the Official Secrets Act (1911). The records of financial transactions are maintained, together with any direct work activity by the board concerned at that address, and is held separately by each board – there are no national records of individual customers. The length of time for which they are kept varies considerably across different boards, but for a minimum of two years before the current year. Thereafter, preservation depends on storage space and the extent of microform facilities.

Records of defaulters, however, will be kept much longer.

Boards will record a change of address only in certain circumstances. It will be requested, for example, if removal occurs before an account is settled, or where a meter has to be read on a specific date. However, any application from an old address to open an account at a new one will be held on file for the latter, not the former. A record of change of address may be destroyed after a couple of years or kept indefinitely – again it depends on the individual board. These particular records may have restricted access within the staff of a credit controller or equivalent.

All addresses held are regarded as confidential and some officers I have approached would not forward mail for a member of the public, let alone divulge a new address. Most, however, would be prepared to do so, but only if they were convinced that it was in a good cause, which would include the location of a relative, and might wish the letter to be unsealed.

I have found an unwillingness among officials to discuss which institutions are normally provided with data from board files on individual accounts, possibly because rules on such disclosure are not necessarily written into regional instructions. All would give data to the police, and to certain other public bodies (which include the boards of the other public utilities and some local government departments: see, e.g., *New Society*, 25 July 1974). The Salvation Army would not be regarded as a public body. The DHSS often requests information, but does not reciprocate.

With the exception of the first, the basic reason for disclosure is the principle of *exchange*. All boards have their own missing persons – those who abscond leaving debts. (Often they are debtors to more than one board.) It is therefore of interest to pool information about some individuals, and act on a *quid pro quo* basis on others. Usually, the electricity boards seem to have the most useful information. Some boards employ their own full time searchers engaged in tracing absconders who disappear with more than a certain level of debt owing. Like British Telecom, the boards sometimes try to minimise this problem by seeking deposits from anyone in a bad risk category or by encouraging the installation of meters or buying the board's stamps (which is, effectively, paying in advance).

C26—The telephone system

The public telephone system in the UK is the responsibility of British Telecommunications plc (BT), with the interesting exceptions (at the time of writing) of Hull and the Channel Islands. Despite privatisation, the records of BT are still subject to Section 2 of the Official Secrets Act (1911), and oral evidence to the Franks Committee stressed that this protection was necessary as a defence not only against private detectives and debt collectors trying to uncover personal information about subscribers, but far more significantly against any who might attempt to undermine or even control the system through a knowledge of its nodal points.

BT retains the monopoly of providing lines and numbers, and is thus in a position to produce the national system of telephone books for all its telephone areas. The full set of telephone books can normally be seen in public libraries, though a branch library might have copies which are a year or two out of date, and not all have those of the Channel Islands and Eire which are outside the BT orbit. The largest libraries may have directories which are some years old in addition to the modern ones, and BT itself has a historical collection which dates from 1880. The retaining of earlier copies will become much more common when they are taken in microfiche, as opposed to book, form.

Some subscribers, particularly the rich, the famous, the notorious, the paranoid, and those with unpleasant memories of unwelcome calls, take the option of having their name, number and address excluded from the published directories – there is no charge for 'going ex-directory', but a change of number costs £11. About 60,000 subscribers per annum go ex-directory, and are flagged as such in BT's internal area lists used by operators. However, operators are not informed of the numbers, which are kept under lock and key; supervisors have access to ex-directory numbers only in their own areas.

The other major item omitted from the published directories is an index of numbers, an omission which tempts the private detective to use a number of subtle devices for wresting the information from those operators. BT's policy of not publishing numbers in sequence is in order to preserve confidentiality. As with the electoral register in alphabetical order, however, it does not actually do so – it merely makes it very time-consuming to find the name required. In the Channel Islands, both name and number indexes are published without, apparently, any ill effects.

BT's records are held on computer nationally, but each area has access only to data on its own subscribers. The information is held on a customer rental record (normally a computer and manual system in tandem) which includes the subscriber's full name, address, telephone number, BT equipment held, jobs done on the line within the previous twelve months, and other account numbers held by the same person, with address(es). The 'subscriber', the person responsible for paying the bill, is deemed to be the person who first applied for the phone to be installed, not the householder or owner necessarily. Access to this data is restricted on a 'right-of-know' basis, and is probably confined to sales or accounts staff; passwords are required by the individuals concerned.

Changes of address are recorded, both within and across areas, in two circumstances – when the move takes place before settlement of the current account, or if the individual applies to open an account at a second address while still living at the first one. It is for each area to determine for how long the record of change of address is maintained; most seem to keep it for at least twelve months, but few for more than two years, when it is destroyed as confidential waste.

BT's internal manual provides its officials with guidance concerning the organisations which have legitimate access to the data. The police may be given names and addresses (and other information through formal procedures); solicitors seeking information about their own clients; the Post Office Users National Council (now the Office of Telecommunications) when investigating complaints; officials of the emergency services, specifically Fire, Ambulance and the Samaritans; and central and local government departments which have the relevant supporting legislation. Normally, requests for information have to be in writing, and BT can make a charge for the service.

The advantages of such access to BT will be enormously enhanced once the relevant technology of Systems X and Y has enabled the destination and length of each call to be recorded, especially as the caller could be logged against the called, as well as vice versa. Those who distrust the encroachment of the State, for whatever reason, have as much cause to fear this development as any other in this book. Such action would not impinge upon the rules governing phone-tapping, the legal basis of which is a warrant issued by the Home Secretary, and undertaken by usually the police, the security services, or HM Customs & Excise, and, much less, by the Post Office and other government departments (see Young, 1978). The last figure made public was 352 per annum (1984), and the procedures have recently been updated by the Interception of Communications Act (over 6,000 warrants were issued in the fifteen years from 1970 to 1984). New numbers will be given over the telephone only if the name and new address of the new subscriber can be supplied – not, for example to requests such as 'please let me have the numbers of all restaurants which have opened in Birmingham in the last twelve months'. BT will not forward mail for anyone requesting such a service; nor does it operate a phone-in facility for teenagers to reassure parents about their safety; see, however, p. 25. Some local discretion may be allowed in cases of medical emergency (for example, a request from an environmental health officer) or where it is clearly in the interests of the subscriber (e.g. a bank trust company seeking a missing beneficiary), but a decision to release information or (more probably) to contact first the individual being sought, could be taken at a fairly high level within the area.

Even though BT could be a major arm of surveillance by the State, and despite a reputation for making substantial profits, it nevertheless finds itself owed large sums of money (perhaps the equivalent of a month's profit), and some of this bad debt is from absconders. Certain precautions are made against this eventuality; customers have to pay for the hire of equipment in advance, and certain people in bad risk groups – students and deserted spouses, for example – may be asked to pay an extra deposit. Many absconders hide from other institutions also, and there is some collaboration on the *quid pro quo* basis between BT and gas and electricity boards, as well as some local authority departments, during a search for these particular missing persons.

C27—Television licensing and rental records

Since 1974, the National Television Licence Records Office at Bristol has operated a computerised system under the direction of the Home Office. Its main purpose is the effective collection of fees, and for that, an up-to-date list of all licence-holders would appear to be necessary; any householder failing to buy a licence receives at least one reminder, and possibly a visit from an investigator and/or a detector van, to see if you are using an unlicensed set (see *New Scientist*, 14 November 1974).

However, the listing is by address rather than by person, and the basis of the licence number is the postcode plus house number, ending with the surname of the licence-holder. Changes of address during the period of a licence may be recorded; but once a new licence is taken out, the former address is not maintained, and the name of the former licence-holder is not kept against the old address. Reminders are sent to 'the occupant', rather than to a named individual.

Television licence records, therefore, will be of little or no help to anyone tracing missing persons, and are, of course, subject to the normal confidentiality of Section 2 of the Official Secrets Act (1911).

The number of customers of individual television rental firms is not published, for commercial reasons. However, market research suggests that over eight million families rent their set; sales of colour sets in 1981 were 1.2 million to the retail trade and 1.1 million to rental firms. The companies' showrooms in shopping areas sometimes maintain records of their own clients, including full name and address, occupation, probably how long with present employer and at current address, telephone number, terms of hire and equipment involved, signature, details of two referees, and the bank and branches if payment is by direct debit. Other firms list their clients centrally, the showroom acting as a convenient point for receipt of fees. An account number is issued chronologically to each client – it will probably have no intrinsic meaning. These details on the original contract will be maintained at the company's headquarters on computer, the record being accessed by name, address or account number. Former addresses will be recorded only at headquarters, and possibly only the address at the time of the contract.

The branch will keep the records for only so long as the customer remains with the firm; headquarters will keep it for some time – months, perhaps even years – depending on whether the individual company has microfilmed them: manual and computer records are destroyed earlier.

I know of no national company which has a specific policy relating to the forwarding of mail – it will be at the individual branch or regional manager's discretion. Some branches have a terminal to the national computer; but most would have to obtain the address of a client of another branch by ringing a regional or national office, quoting their own branch code number.

In common with so many other institutions, some television rental companies have no written instructions about access to records by outside bodies; others specifically confine the divulging of information to the police only. They are bound to inform the Licensing Centre at Bristol of the names and addresses of each new customer (though, strangely enough, this is only relating to television hire, not video). It is unlikely that anyone other than the police would be given a client's address officially; it is, of course, in the interest of any manager to maintain co-operation with the agency so largely involved in recovering stolen property.

All such companies have their own 'missing person' problems with absconding defaulters. After preliminary attempts by the firm to locate these individuals, the task is normally handed over to a private enquiry agent.

C28—Premium bonds

Premium bonds, held by almost half the population of the country, are the responsibility of the Bonds and Stock Office at Lytham St Annes, part of the Department for National Savings. As such, the staff are subject to the Official Secrets Acts and statutory regulations, as well as internal discipline which militates against disclosure of confidential information.

Two numbers are involved. The meaning of the bond number itself is described in the leaflet 'Twenty Questions on ERNIE', the initial letter denoting the denomination of the bond and the remainder merely a chronological issue. More important from our point of view is the computerised Holder's Number. This number, unique to the holder, is like an account number. It consists of eight digits (because of the large number of bondholders) and a letter which is a check character (designed to eliminate errors in transcription of the eight digits).

Premium bond purchase application forms ask for the Holder's Number, or if not known, whether the purchaser already holds bonds. It is evident, therefore, that the Bonds and Stock Office has the facility for listing bondholders in alphabetical and Holder's Number order, together with the bond numbers held. The Office can therefore check how many bonds an individual holds – a maximum of £10,000 is allowed at present. The files record the bondholder's address at the time of purchase and all subsequent changes of address notified to the Office, and are maintained until all the holder's bonds are cashed.

Potentially, therefore, the Bonds and Stock Office is an enormous source of information on the location of individuals, but cannot be used as such because of the nature of its statutory regulations. Staff are, however, occasionally asked to trace missing relatives and although they have a policy of not supplying personal details, such as current addresses, they are sympathetic towards *genuine anxiety* and will forward a letter from the relative to the bondholder. Generally they do not undertake to help any official body, including the police, in tracing missing persons. Solicitors, attornies and accountants officially acting on behalf and with the authority of the bondholder, also receivers, are the only individuals outside the Office allowed information from an individual's file.

The reason for this policy is to maintain the confidence of bondholders by ensuring that details of their holdings, whereabouts, etc., will remain confidential. Premum bond winners are notified at their last-known address. The winning bond numbers for the higher value prizes are published in the press. All prizewinning numbers appear monthly in the *London Gazette Supplement* which, four times a year, also includes the numbers of unclaimed prizewinners. Despite this publicity, and there being no time limit for paying out, a total of about £2.5 million in prize money (including some prizes of £5,000) have not been collected by approximately 45,000 prizewinners. (This, however, represents only 0.2 per cent of the total number of prizes issued since the start of the scheme.) In most cases the missing prizewinners will have simply moved house without notifying ERNIE; others could be deceased and their executors have not notified the death, and in a few cases the names of the winners are not known. The Bonds and Stock Office tries to locate these missing persons through their selling agents, the Post Office, and banks. As in the case of bank trust companies, their search must be impaired by being unable to divulge the purpose of the enquiry to unauthorised persons.

If you have changed your address and not notified the Bonds and Stock Office you could be one of the 45,000. You should complete your Holder's Card stating your new address and send it to them. If the card is missing ask for form P2767B at the Post Office. If you have lost your bonds tell them, and replacement certificates will be issued. Any outstanding prizes due will automatically be sent to you.

C29—The drivers register

Licences to drive motorised vehicles in England, Scotland and Wales are issued by the Department of Transport, via the Driver and Vehicle Licensing Centre (DVLC) at Swansea, whose records are therefore subject to Section 2 of the Official Secrets Act (1911). Some thirty-seven million names are included on the register, with seventy-two per cent of all eligible males and thirty-one per cent of all eligible females holding a full driving licence in 1983. The information on the register is computerised, and access is confined to the DVLC.

Initial data is received from the licence application form, which is retained on microfilm. The applicant must make a signed application giving full name, title, address, sex, date of birth, details of previous licence held, driving offences, and brief details of any medical condition (including visual, physical and mental defects) which might affect his ability to drive safely. He must also state whether he has previously been refused a licence on medical grounds. Signature, date, and cheque or postal order number must also be supplied. The licence itself instructs drivers to inform the DVLC whenever a change of name or address occurs. The courts can impose a fine of up to £400 on anyone convicted of failing to do so. Additionally, information is fed in by the police, the courts, and by other sections of the Department of Transport, so details of current endorsements and disqualifications are also recorded.

Not all of the thirty-seven million records on the drivers register relate to *current* licence-holders. There is, for example, no way in which the DVLC is automatically informed of the death of a licence-holder, so reliance for this information is placed on the next of kin, solicitors and executors; also, endorsements ordered by court are in force for some, and in any case, entitlement to renew a full licence remains for ten years from the date of expiry.

Upon successful completion of a driving test, a driver can apply for a full licence (normally valid until the day before the seventieth birthday). The first licence issued will contain the driver's date of birth; on each licence, however, will be the Driver Number which normally stays the same on any future one. The Driver Number is the key to finding a driver's record, and is in three sections. The first consists of the first five letters of the surname; the second is the date of birth in coded form, the first and sixth digit being the year, the second and third the month, and the fourth and fifth the day; (female drivers have five added to the second digit). The third consists of the initial letters of the first two fornames; a nine, unless anyone else of the same names and date of birth has already been issued with a licence; and finally two letters which act as a computer check digit. Any blank in the name or initials section will be filled with a nine, and the last three characters in the number ensure that the Driver Number is unique to the individual driver.

In addition to using the Driver Number to locate a driver's record, it is therefore possible to trace a record if the full name and date of birth are known. Access to the Drivers Register is strictly controlled for reasons of privacy, and information from it is provided only to authorised users – mainly law enforcement agencies, and the driver himself. In 1983, of 1.3 million disclosures, 950,000 were to the police, 300,000 to the DVLC itself and other government departments (principally Customs & Excise and Inland Revenue), and 50,000 to other sections of the Department of Transport and licensing authorities. Data is disclosed only in response to enquiries about driver licensing, road safety, enforcements, and the prevention and detection of crime. Other parties may receive information only with the consent of the drivers concerned.

Although the ability to create a Driver's Number when one is not known, combined with the computerisation of such large numbers of entries, give this system enormous potential for tracing missing persons, the DVLC is in a position similar to the Inland Revenue when it comes to helping enquirers by forwarding unaddressed mail: they are not staffed to undertake this work, and would only do so for very good reasons (which should be given, with the one letter to be forwarded). The DVLC will not act as a post office for two parties, or forward mail for trivial reasons. The letter to be forwarded should be unsealed, as the Centre is anxious not to be party to any communication which might cause offence. Requests should be sent to Fee Paying Enquiries, DVLC, Swansea SA99 1AN.

C30—The Vehicle Register

The Driver and Vehicle Licensing Centre (DVLC) at Swansea, part of the Department of Transport, is responsible for maintaining a register of the keepers of motorised vehicles in England, Scotland and Wales, so that that the State can ensure that the excise duty payable on such vehicles is collected and also facilitate law enforcement and road safety. The records are covered, therefore, by Section 2 of the Official Secrets Act (1911).

Access to the DVLC register of vehicle-keepers is only by the vehicle registration number. The data held are supplied by the registered keepers themselves, who may or may not be the vehicle owners. The vehicle registration document has provision whereby a change of name or address can be notified to the DVLC, the penalty for failing to do so being currently £100.

Registration of the vehicle itself is by a series of letters and numbers on a principle similar to that of the National Health Service Number (see pp. 53–4): it contains a reference to the place and date of initial registration, and has a pattern which changes every few years. Registration numbers on military vehicles are not included, being issued by the Ministry of Defence. Unlike the NHS codes, however, car registration codes have (with few exceptions) been published, and may be bought in the form of spotters' guides.

The full name, title, company (if applicable), address and signature are recorded about the keeper, and the taxation class, make, model, colour, type of fuel, registration number, Vehicle Identification Number, engine number, cylinder capacity, date of registration and reference to earlier keepers are recorded about the vehicle.

An abbreviated version of this data is fed daily into the Police National Computer as a now indispensable facility for crime detection (see p. 138). A search for missing persons in connection with vehicle registration is also very often a civil matter, arising from the need to identify the driver or owner of a vehicle whose number has already been obtained, perhaps as a result of a minor accident or an infringement of private parking rights, for example. Under Regulation 15 of the Road Vehicles (Registration and Licensing) Regulations 1971, made under the Vehicle (Excise) Act of the same year, information from the Vehicle Register can be given by the DVLC to the police, government departments, local authorities in connection with offences, and to any member of the public who can show a 'reasonable cause'. In practice, this phrase is interpreted as involving the vehicle itself (not simply the keeper) in matters to do with criminal law, or road safety. All enquiries are logged, and checked against these criteria; the DVLC estimates that about fifty requests per week are rejected. The current fee is £2.

In 1983, the estimated number of disclosures from the Vehicle

Register's 33,673,000 entries was about five million, with the following breakdown:

Central Ticket Office	2,818,000
Local authorities	1,166,000
Vehicle manufacturers (safety recalls)	550,000
Police	393,000
Insurance companies	45,000
Other government departments	30,000
Registered keepers and owners	30,000
General public	25,000
Solicitors	8,000
Non-governmental 'enforcement agencies', e.g. the RSPCA	3,000

The possible use of the Vehicle Register for forwarding unaddressed mail to missing persons is as described on p. 136 for persons on the Drivers Register.

C31—The Police National Computer

The largest of the many computer systems available to police forces in Britain, the Police National Computer (PNC) has been operated by the Home Office at Hendon since 1974. It holds data in a series of indexes (a somewhat misleading term, in this case) which can be accessed by several hundred terminals held by force headquarters and by some divisions; as yet, fewer than half the forces can also interface it with their own computer systems. The growth in the use of the PNC over the last few years is an indication of its great utility to police enquiries, as well as to an increasing awareness among officers as to its potential. Even as late as 1983, however, an article in *Police Review* could still refer to it as being to most officers 'a mysterious a piece of technology as the flight-deck of the Starship Enterprise'. In that year, nevertheless, it was used on thirty-one million occasions in enquiries relating to its forty-three million entries. Its use has been of some concern to those anxious about civil liberties (see, for example, Pounder, 1985).

By far the largest section on the PNC is the Vehicle Owners Index, with over thirty-five million entries updated daily from the DVLC (see p. 137). It contains on each car the name, address, and postcode of the registered keeper, date of registration, and the registration, chassis and engine number, model, colour, and make of most vehicles, though not those registered in the Isle of Man or the Channel Islands, military vehicles or trade plates. On-line access is by the registration number itself, but records can be searched on combinations of descriptive factors or partial registration numbers; such searches have to be authorised by a senior police officer, and carried out at the Computer Centre. Vehicle checking may be at random, but the automatic number plate reader, with which the Home Office was experimenting in 1983, has now been abandoned.

Two other indexes relating to vehicles concern stolen chassis and engine numbers, and a list of stolen or suspect vehicles. The former, with 542,713 entries at 18 May 1985, contains Vehicle Identification Numbers which can be cross-referenced to the stolen vehicles file in order, for example, to reveal false number plates. Several other engines (marine, cement mixers, and so on) are included. The stolen and suspect vehicles index, with almost half a million entries, lists the registered keepers and brief description of vehicles, updated from force terminals. It includes vehicles which are lost or stolen (256,943), found or abandoned (23,095), obtained by deception (553), repossessed (93), suspected of being used in a crime (3,140), removed to the police car pound (10,322), removed by the police to another street (294), used for police purposes (6,296), and three vaguer categories – long-term interest to the police (35,094), seen or checked in noteworthy circumstances (11,647), and 'blocked' (3,855) (figures as at 1 June 1985). The penultimate category appears to be used for a variety of circumstances, including the vehicles of miners' pickets during the 1984/85 strike; the significance of the last has not been acknowledged, and may be the listing of the vehicles of the Special Branch and Security Services.

Three other files refer to people rather than vehicles, and are called the Names Indexes. They all include name, age, sex, colour and height, and warning signals which indicate conditions which may affect the health or safety of anyone directly involved in an investigation; they include references to known drugs taken, alcoholism or ailments, for example. There were 4,974,479 entries in the Criminal Names Index at 18 May 1985, entered by the National Identification Bureau in New Scotland Yard, but accessed as usual by all terminals. It contains the above data, including known aliases and Criminal Records Office Number, of all persons convicted of (or awaiting trial for) a serious offence, but details of convictions, crime and method are yet to be incorporated. The CRO Number is a straightforward chronological allocation within a specified year, plus a computer check digit.

The Disqualified Drivers Index (298,436 entries in 1985) also includes aliases, date of birth, address, any Criminal Record Number, the DVLC Driver Number, disqualification period, and court code. The record is deleted at the end of the disqualification period. The Index does not include suspended or revoked licences.

Finally, and most pertinently, an Index of Wanted and Missing Persons was started in 1978. It includes individuals who are wanted, missing, found, suspected, deserters, absconders, witnesses required, and those who fail to appear at court or who are recalled to prison or Borstal. It is updated, as well as accessed, by the teriminals, and includes a reference to any Criminal Record Reference Number, with a very brief description of no more than 13 seven-letter words about the person or acquaintance(s). Most entries relate to those who are being sought for specific charges or unresolved enquiries (109,659 on 18 May 1985, compared with 65,000 in January 1979). Unidentified individuals, at the point of enquiry, totalled only seventeen and those who were 'missing' and might be vulnerable to harm, or believed to be in the company of such a missing person, numbered 2,089. Entries are deleted when the person is found and (where appropriate) returned, though others may be stored on the computer for periods which vary according to the case. Entries for missing persons are accessed either by name or by 'WM' (Wanted/Missing) Number which is allocated by the PNC to each reported case – the number consists of two digits indicating the year followed by a chronological allocation and a computer check digit. Over 240,000 were issued in 1984 alone. I suspect that national statistics of missing persons could be produced by the Home Office if, in contrast to other categories in this Index, those who are simply reported missing could be distinguished by being given, for example, an even WM number.

It is evident, nevertheless, that not all persons reported missing are entered on the PNC. Forces issue their own instructions on the situation as part of their written standing orders and do not act within a national directive. One Welsh force, for example, forwards details of persons regarded as vulnerable if they are missing for fourteen days; one English force enters all missing persons on the PNC unless the police have reason to believe that they will be located within a short period. Whereas the PNC may be a useful aid for the identification of missing persons, once located, the numbers entered in this Index cannot be taken as a completely reliable statistical guide for national totals or even trends.

A single enquiry can elicit data from more than one index, and such multiple referencing can produce quite unexpected results. One man, having called in the police to report that his music centre had been stolen, was arrested for having been an army deserter twenty-two years earlier. There are separate facilities for transmitting messages between forces, and for fingerprint enquiries now that over three and a half million prints have been computerised.

There is a code of practice for the protection of personal data held on the PNC which requires all forces to carry out regular checks on the use of computer transactions, and on the accuracy of certain types of records. In the early years of the PNC, the system appears to have been abused by some ex-policemen who understood its potential. This problem has now been minimised, particularly by the logging of each request for six months by the PNC. Nevertheless, those with friends still on the Force have thereby *potential* access to a colossal amount of information to help with private enquires (for a detective agency or private firm, for example), an advantage which some would find hard to ignore. The enormous number of legitimate enquiries means that proactive checking is virtually impossible, but such divulging is an offence against Section 2 of the 1911 Official Secrets Act, the Data Protection Act, and Police Discipline Regulations, and officers known to have misused information are dealt with by criminal proceedings if appropriate.

Disclosure of police information, including criminal records, is a matter for chief officers of police but certain bodies outside the police may be legitimately given information – for example, where an individual has applied for a position of trust in a central or local government organisation. The police have also been asked to report to the DES (see p. 92) and DHSS respectively convictions for all but minor offences committed by teachers and others employed in the care of children. Similar reports are made to the governing bodies concerned of convictions of Civil Servants, dentists, doctors, lawyers, midwives, nurses and the staff of the Post Office, British Telecom, the Civil Aviation Authority and the UK Atomic Energy Authority. Character reports may be given to relevant authorities by the police for prospective foster and adoptive parents, and applicants for various licences including those for heavy goods vehicle and passenger service vehicle operators. A recent Home Office/DHSS review has recently (1985) extended the facility for checking the index to criminal records of those who apply for jobs, or who volunteer to work with children in local authorities, the NHS, and (possibly in the future) several hundred voluntary organisations.

C32—The Royal Mail redirection service

The Post Office offers a service for the redirection of mail from one address to another on payment of the appropriate fee. The period can be for one, three or twelve months (the periods of three or twelve months are renewable). Additional postage may however be charged for items being redirected abroad. Redirection takes place at the delivery post office serving the old address. Redirection requests are retained for twelve months after the expiry date of the period paid for by the customer; this is mainly for auditing purposes but is also useful in case of any dispute which might arise concerning the redirection.

It would, of course, make nonsense of this arrangement if the Post Office were to help to locate missing persons by forwarding mail after the requested period of redirection has ended; therefore requests by trade or enquiry agents for addresses are always refused. However, certain official bodies may, in special circumstances, be given redirection addresses on request – for example, a senior police officer enquiring into a serious crime; the Inland Revenue enquiring into tax defaults; the Customs & Excise in respect of a VAT enquiry; an official receiver appointed by the Board of Trade; the 'Race Relations Board' (unless the addressee had specifically requested that the new address be kept confidential), and a Trading Standards Officer acting within the 1968 Trades Descriptions Act. Actual access within the Post Office to the new address is at the local sorting office.

The Post Office's obligation ends when the mail is delivered to the address, not necessarily to the addressee. If the delivery postman knows that the intended recipient is no longer at that address – perhaps through removal or death, and that any items delivered to the address will be returned by the present occupier – or if a forwarding address has been left, the mail will be stopped at the sorting office, and appropriate action taken.

Undeliverable mail is endorsed accordingly and returned unopened to any sender wise enough to have put his own address on the letter or packet. However, where there is no visible return address the mail is passed to a Returned Letter Section where it is opened (there is one such section in each Head Post Office) in order to ascertain the name and address so that it can be returned. Returned letter sections are generally staffed by volunteers on overtime and this often results in a backlog of several weeks' work at offices in large cities. Although this procedure may seem over-cautious, it is only one step removed from the deliberate interception of mail, for which the statutory authority must come from the Home Secretary; about 100 warrants are issued annually for authorised interception, the procedure governed by the Interception of Communications Act (1985).

C33—Hospital records

Drury (1973) and Körner (1982) provide the heads of information which are held now, and with suggestions for change in the future, by NHS hospitals regarding their patients. These records include (in addition to the medical information, which does not concern us here) full names (including any change thereto), address, date of birth, marital status and title, sex, occupation, GP's name and address, consultant and ward, nationality, religion, name, address and telephone number of next of kin, dates of admission and discharge/death, and any hospital number allocated. Hospitals are free to devise their own data collection forms, and the information listed above is sometimes supplemented by, for example, place of birth, occupation of spouse, whether the patient is in receipt of a pension, and maiden name.

The obvious omission from this list is the NHS Number which, after all, helps to establish the patient's right to treatment, and in practice I found that all but one of the hospitals visited for this book did try to record it. Their evident lack of success (despite the fact that the GP ought to have been able to supply it) can lead to problems of identification, and this in turn has led many Regional Health Authorities to devise their own patient identification number, sometimes based on date of birth. Benjamin (1980) goes further, advocating a national identification number. Körner (1982), however, has not recommended the compulsory recording of such a system, concluding 'We reluctantly accept that in the forseeable future there is no prospect of a national number being used universally but would like to encourage local experiments with the use of the NHS number.' The main source of the problem was that so few people appeared to know their own number, and Körner suggests that it should be recorded only in the case of babies born in hospital.

All hospitals visited kept manual files, but had varying degrees of computerisation in addition. One, indeed, was involved in the Tay-side system for linking FPC and hospital records by this means, though this does not include medical details (see Angus et al., 1978). Computer records are such a recent development that none reported to me had been culled without leaving some manual record for future reference.

Each hospital keeps its own records on behalf of the Secretary of State; they must conform to the Public Records Acts and be kept for a minimum length of time laid down by the DHSS. This is eight years for records of adults, and until the age of twenty-five for minors. (For fuller details, see DHSS Health Circular (80)7, May 1980). Medical records in private hospitals are owned by the consultants (and, it seems, permanently borrowed by them for private patients in NHS hospitals), but the NHS also insists that an admission book and daily theatre book are kept by the private hospital concerned. In practice, both types of hospital keep their records for much longer than this minimum, the period being determined by storage space, microform facilities, and the willingness to deposit under the 100-year confidentiality rule: the hospitals visited varied from two to seventy years above the minimum. Once into long-term storage, the records are sometimes maintained in nominal alphabetical order, though this is unneccessary with a Master Patient Index system.

In common with other sectors of the NHS, hospitals treat non-medical data with the same confidentiality as details of illness and treatment. Nevertheless, they are usually willing to forward mail to enquirers, and frequently do so for individuals trying to re-establish contact with friends made on the wards. If you are in this position, you should write to the Medical Records Officer (MRO) of the hospital concerned, enclosing a sealed letter to be forwarded, and the name, date of hospitalisation, and ward of the individual concerned – date of birth would be even better, but it is unlikely that you would know it. Out of courtesy, the MRO should be told of the reason for the request, though none told me that this would be a requirement. It will be remarked that the willingness of MROs to forward *sealed* mail is relatively unusual among NHS staff. Normally, the interests of patients' welfare are such that they are shielded to a high degree, and they are protected from the receipt of bad news, offensive messages, or unsolicited advertising. My impression is that MROs do not regard *former* patients as needing such protection.

At the time of writing, the DHSS is preparing guidance which will control access to data held by the NHS which has been the subject of a report by Mrs Körner's steering group of Health Services information (see Körner, 1984). Health Authorities have been asked to comment on whether there should by any differentiation between manual and computerised data. The draft maintains the principle that all data (including a patient's address) are held for medical purposes, and would be divulged to persons outside the NHS only in defined circumstances (see below). The craft code is reproduced in Körner, 1984.

Release of patient data within the NHS is normally through the staff of the MRO, via computer passwords or keys to the relevant filing cabinets. Any unusual request for access – to undertake research, for example – might also involve the hospital administrator, legal advisers, the doctors' ethical committee, and always the consultant in charge of the individual case(s). On the other hand, MRO staff sometimes give data over the phone to other doctors in the same hospital, and this practice is potentially a much greater security risk than the passing out of patients' files to medical staff with an accompanying receipt.

The proposed guidance regarding confidentiality of patient data held by the NHS will codify what is already common practice, though as Körner (1984) notes, there are variations across hospitals and regions. Superimposed upon the general principle that data should be used only in connection with the purposes for which it was collected in the first place are certain exceptions in which the law or the public interest is deemed to override this confidentiality. So, of course, will the needs of auditors. All other divulging should be only with the consent of the patients concerned.

The code requires that information must be given, with or without that consent, in accordance with various legislation relating to public health, abortion, health and safety, mental health, and the NHS, together with their relevant regulations. Courts of law and some tribunals can order disclosure, as can health authorities investigating complaints. The prevention or detection of serious crime may also justify disclosure. National security may also require the same response, though only at the signed request of a cabinet minister, the Attorney-General, or Lord Advocate (see Körner, 1984, for a comprehensive list).

At the moment, relationships with the police vary from one hospital to another, as guidance leaves some latitude in the hands of the MRO and Administrator. 'Serious crime' is not defined, and is certainly not restricted to the work of the police Serious Crime Squad (see Section 116 of the Police and Criminal Evidence Act, 1984). The new code should help to clarify what has been a grey area for many MROs, however, some of whom have the benefit of a hospital security officer (usually an ex-policeman) through whom an approach is made in cases where the public interest is thought to be paramount. I have found considerable suspicion of police motives, and some alienation resulting from police methods, among MROs, and the BMA had to protest about the abuse of police access to data during an NHS fraud investigation which was thought to infringe the agreed BMA/ACPO joint statement of 1980 (see *The Guardian*, 15 June 1984). Certainly an MRO is much more likely to provide data about persons whose identities are already known to the police rather than supplying the names and addresses of, for example, anyone treated for certain injuries within a specified period. When the police are involved – whether looking for suspects or witnesses – a decision about release of data would be referred to the hospital Administrator.

MROs are faced with many other requests from outside the NHS for personal patient data. Journalists are interested in the medical progress of the famous and the infamous, the relationship between hospitals and the Press still being governed by a Ministry of Health circular from 1956 which reconciled the public interest with the confidentiality of different groups of patients; employers test the veracity of employees' reasons for absence; husbands want to know the time of their wife's appointments; and so on. No guidance is given by their professional body (the Association of Health Care Information and Medical Records Officers), but the varying reactions to requests from outside bodies should once again be standardised by legislation. Most MROs divulge nothing to persons outside the NHS and police, but some have indicated that they would respond helpfully to enquiries from the DHSS and Customs & Excise, and might *confirm* data for the Salvation Army. All, however, remember the consequences of revealing, apparently innocently, information about the death of a patient, only to learn later that it had been abused to give a new identity to a famous MP.

C34—Removal firms

As with firms of employers generally, removal firms vary considerably in size, from the nationally-known to the small-town, and once again size has some influence on how long records are kept, and who has access to the data therein. The British Association of Removers appears to have issued no guidelines about confidentiality, though there has been some correspondence on the issue in its journal. Practices therefore vary, and this should be borne in mind when reading the generalisations which follow.

Removal firms draw up an initial contract with a client, containing a relatively full job description. This should be kept for six years, though one firm interviewed kept them for five. There is also a day book or log, indicating chronologically the name of each client, the two addresses involved, the quantity of goods to be moved, the cost, and any provisos relating to unusual circumstances. The firm would know, in most cases, whether emigration had been intended, and will often have been paid by cheque, thus having another point of reference to the client for at least six years (see pp. 75–6). The day books are kept much longer than the contracts, twenty years and more in some cases, and are usually discarded only because of pressure on space. Large firms hold the records at branch level only, and (to my knowledge) do not computerise them. They can be indexed by address, or name, or job number, a facility not really needed by small firms.

There is no simple way to know which firm has been used to effect a removal, and recently there has been a growth in the use of self-hire vans for the purpose. The likelihood is that the best known, or the nearest to current *or new* address will have been employed, gleaned from the Yellow Pages. Most firms appear to be willing to forward unaddressed mail to former clients, though one or two said that it would have to be a 'deserving case'.

It is generally in the firms' own interests to protect the clients' assumed desire for confidentiality, and most requests for new addresses would be refused: they might, however, inform the client that, for example, the Salvation Army, a bank, or a solicitor was trying to get in touch with them. Only the police, the Inland Revenue, or the

Customs & Excise could expect to be given access to data, and that only in person and with proof of identity. There is scope, however, for firms to be hoodwinked by the hard luck story, and in the case of small firms, the owner has daily access to the record and can decide for himself how it is to be used.

Complaints relayed to me from removal firms related not to private detectives but to their local gas boards. In one case, a firm had assisted the board with their own enquiries in the past, which had refused to reciprocate when the removal firm asked for help in tracing one of its bad debtors. Another had given a new address to the long-lost relative of a client, only to discover later that he was really a gas board official. Experiences such as these make firms wary of helping anyone directly, but if the client is known to have defrauded, or simply be in debt to, another local business, then it is probable that the business interest would be put before the client's privacy.

C35—Passports

Although the holding of a passport is not necessary in order to leave this country, it *is* a necessity for entry into most others. In practice, therefore, the knowledge of whether a passport has been issued is a normal first step in discovering whether someone has left the country.

No citizen is automatically entitled to a passport, and there are some well-defined cases for whom one might be refused, e.g. minors, whose journey might be in contrary to a court order, to the wishes of parents or those with custody or care and control, or to certain statutory provisions; persons for whose arrest a warrant has been issued; those whose past activities lead the authorities to believe that the issuing of a passport would not be in the public interest (a refusal exercised very rarely); and British nationals repatriated at public expense if they have not yet paid their debts.

UK passports are issued under the Royal Prerogative to British nationals who are able to establish national status and identity. Responsibility for issuing them in the UK was transferred to the Home Office in 1984, and Section 2 of the Official Secrets Act (1911) applies to the relevant documents. In England and Wales there are four Passport Offices (at Liverpool, London, Newport and Peterborough) to which applications are directed on a regional basis (see current application forms for addresses).

The extent of the family data submitted on the application form is greater than on any other document in this book, even including the census. Full name, address, maiden name, marital status, town and country of birth, telephone number, occupation, date of birth, height, distinguishing marks, change of name, citizenship status, previous passports held, photograph, details of the countersignatory, birth certificate, marriage certificate or divorce decree, countries to be visited, purpose of journey, names, addresses, telephone numbers and relationship of two relatives or friends, and the applicant's dated signature, are all recorded. The countersignatory is the system's main defence against misuse of the passport facility by those who may wish to obtain one in a false identity. The Home Office is sufficiently aware of the factual abuse in the affair of John Stonehouse, and the fictional ploy in Frederick Forsyth's novel *The Day of the Jackal*, to have instituted a series of checks, and there have been many successful prosecutions of such offences, so that the Home Office belives that successful abuse of the countersignatory system is extremely rare. Six people were sentenced at the Old Bailey in October, 1985 for this offence.

The original application forms are retained for only eleven years, the passport itself being valid for no more than ten, and are then almost all destroyed. The Passport Department of the Home Office has records relating to passports issued back in 1890, and a constant index is maintained which survives the destruction of the application forms, whose location and indexing system during those eleven years are classified. A brief entry of each passport issued in the UK is also made in passport registers, which are transferred to the Public Record Office and made available for public inspection when they are thirty years old. These registers are arranged in chronological order, and show only the date, the number of the passport issued, and the surname and initials of the applicant. The interpretation of the number (preceded by a letter normally representing the issuing office, the final letter ensuring that the same number is not issued twice within a ten-year period) is also classified; the same individual will not always be reissued with the same number.

There is no direct link between the Passport Offices and immigration, so that the former will not know whether a particular passport, once issued, has actually been used for international travel. Other departments, however, have a professional interest in keeping watch on the movements of individuals if they are suspected of criminal activity, and the effectiveness of this surveillance will be considerably enhanced when the new passport, planned to be issued from 1987 in a format common to other EEC countries, is introduced. The data it contains – name, nationality, date of birth, sex, passport number, date of expiry and a check digit – can all be read by the passport holder and by machine so that there will be a significant reduction in the time taken to process the movement of passengers.

Access to the application forms during their eleven years in existence is restricted to government departments and to the police on a need-to-know basis. However, any member of the public, upon payment of a fee (currently £7) can be informed if a specified person, whose full name and date of birth are supplied, holds a current passport. Application for this information may be made to any of the Passport Offices, giving the reason for the request. Most of the enquiries relate to tracing missing persons, or assisting with genealogical research.

C36—Holiday and travel records

Most holiday companies operate through travel agents, and it is the latter who hold records of holiday-makers. There are a few firms, however, which combine both functions, selling holidays to the public direct.

Travel agents will preserve a record of clients not merely in connection with current holidays but also to support future marketing projects. They usually keep such a record for at least three years, many firms for as long as seven. Record is kept of names and addresses (or at least one for contact in the case of party holidays), date of travel, destination, tour company, telephone number, age (especially of children), means of payment, and any infirmity if the data had been supplied. Some firms keep a full file on each holiday-maker for a few years, in case of complaints or later court action; thereafter only names and addresses. Any number allocated to an individual holiday-maker is likely to have nothing more than the year encoded into it.

Holiday firms are used to receiving enquiries as to the home address of holiday-makers over such innocuous matters as photographs, and will forward sealed mail if accompanied by a reasonable explanation for the request. One or two prefer to contact the client themselves, asking them to get in touch with enquirers.

Firms vary considerably not only in the length for which records are kept, but also in conditions of storage. In some offices, all employees can have access to all data. In others, only the current year's information is given, earlier data being accessed through a supervisor.

Employees are trained to respect the confidentiality of a client's record, but practices concerning disclosure again vary from firm to firm. The police will be given information without a warrant, especially if the request is signed by a senior officer to ensure that it is not a matter personal to the constable concerned. Some would provide data to the DHSS, especially if it is a matter of confirming dates and cost; a few would help a local authority or the Salvation Army, though most would merely forward a letter for them. They are particularly wary of telephone enquiries, particularly those innocently asking for 'my wife's time of departure/arrival'.

Travel firms such as Thomas Cook, which are now selling millions of tickets each year, no longer maintain a record of such transactions, but airlines do. In their case, however, only name and a contact phone number are recorded, not the exact address. Either the reservations or the completed flight coupons are stored for three months (British Caledonian) to six months (British Airways), each of which require a court order for anyone other than certain authorities to have access to the data. There are, however, detailed procedures laid down to cope with emergencies or accidents; where appropriate, British Caledonian, for example, would disclose information to the Civil Aviation Authority, the police, HM Customs & Excise, or to a member of the legal profession.

Neither airline is prepared to forward mail to former passengers.

C37—Hotel records

Hotels, whether of international standards or back-street lodging-houses, keep some record of their guests, most of whom are short-stay visitors, though there are well over 40,000 families being semi-permanently housed therein by local authorities. Each hotel can decide for itself what information to record. With the exceptions of guests aged under sixteen, and those exempted by the Diplomatic Privileges Act of 1964, the law lays down a minimum amount of data to be recorded on each – name, date of arrival, nationality, and (in the case of aliens), the intended next destination. (Commonwealth citizens, persons from British Protectorates, and those serving with NATO and UK forces are treated as though they were British citizens for this purpose, and citizens of Common Market countries may soon be in the same position.)

Normally, a registration card preserves the full name and address, date of arrival and departure, and room number. The signature of the paper is also recorded, but (in the case of the YMCA at least, where the minimum age for guests is sixteen), this appears to be voluntary. Confirmations may also be kept for quite a long time, in order to facilitate investigation of subsequent enquiries about the bill. Passport numbers of aliens will also be recorded, the normal document required for proof of identity. For Britons, no proof of identity (or of age, for that matter) is required, and one of the problems facing detectives investigating the Brighton Grand Hotel bombing in 1984 was the number of guests who had stayed at the hotel under assumed identities.

Other countries, particularly the USA and Japan, have now introduced a more technologically-advanced system of recording, in which registers and record cards have been replaced by a computer-linked card system which not only records data automatically when used, but also opens the hotel room door. It seems probable that such innovations will be adopted here shortly.

The length of time for which hotel records are kept varies considerably above the twelve months' minimum required by law. The BTH chain, for example, keeps records for two years; others keep them for much longer, or have no policy for disposal.

The forwarding of mail to former guests is sometimes requested, and usually complied with; no reason is normally sought, and no stipulation will be made about leaving the letter unsealed. The larger hotels will want a fairly exact date on which the intended recipient had been a guest, and possibly even the room number.

Reception staff and management normally have access to the hotel's guest records, and Statutory Instrument 1689, the Immigration (Hotel Records) Order 1972, opens them to any police constable, or to any person authorised by the Secretary of State. In principle, and often in practice, they are kept confidential from all other enquirers. However, the smaller hotels in particular may be easily tempted by requests for information from other persons.

C38—Divorce

Case records are maintained at the County or High Court where the divorce proceedings were heard; if the result is a decree absolute, copies of the final certificate may be obtained, in person or by post, by any member of the public. This decree absolute includes the names of the two parties, the date and place of the marriage being terminated, and the name of any co-respondent. Most of the records, however, including details of the hearing, dates of birth of children to the marriage, and the final settlement, are confidential to the two parties concerned, their solicitors, or to anyone to whom the Official Secrets Acts apply, when they are on legitimate business. (Despite this, it may be worth making an approach to the court for access if you can show that the parties have given permission, or are dead.) The files are kept for at least fifty years and may then be, with a few exceptions, destroyed.

A record of all decrees absolute since 1857 is held by the Record Keeper of the Divorce Registry at Somerset House, through whom copies may be obtained. There is a fee of £2.25 for a search of three years in the indexes, and the full names of both spouses must be supplied; there will be a delay of a few days because the copy will be issued by the court in which the proceedings had taken place. There are no geographical boundaries to the jurisdiction of each court, so it is by no means obvious where the case was heard; the index at Somerset House, however, covers the whole of England and Wales.

It seems extraordinary that, whereas indexes of marriage are made public, those of divorce are not, and it seems to me that a good social case can be made for divorce being registered and indexed also by the Registrar-General, in order to make public the death of a marriage as well as its birth.

It can happen that a petitioner wishes to divorce a spouse whose whereabouts are unknown. If more than seven years have elapsed since the disappearance, a mechanism involving legal presumption of death is available (see p. 41). However, the onus to locate the missing person lies with the petitioner, whose solicitor might employ a private detective for the search and process serving, or might request the services of the court bailiff for the same. The process server tries to obtain the signature and place of receipt (usually the residence or place of employment) on a court document by which receipt of the copy of the petition, and identity, are acknowledged.

If, however, the respondent cannot be traced, the courts will wish to be satisfied that all reasonable steps to make contact have been taken – letters to known living relatives, to DHSS Central Records, to the respondent's bank, and so on. If there is any indication of emigration, an advertisement should be placed in an appropriate national newspaper. Affidavits concerning these attempts to make contact will be required by the court which will then determine how best to proceed on the evidence presented in each case.

C39—Emigration

No central or local government department in Britain automatically records the fact of emigration, and as a result it is often very difficult to know whether a missing person has left the country. As we have seen, it is easy to find out if an individual has been issued with a passport (see p. 150), but neither the Passport Office nor other sections of the Home Office (whose potential oversight of emigration would be processed, oddly enough, by its immigration officers) normally record the use which all passport holders make of this facility. Figures for emigration statistics since 1961, produced by the OPCS, are grossed up estimates from interviews for the International Passenger Survey (IPS) (now following recommendations of the United Nations Statistical Commission in 1976), and the names of the individuals in the sample used are not recorded.

In consequence, a search of various documentary sources may have to be undertaken in order to prove that someone has emigrated, and even then there is no certainty that the individual will be traced even if he is travelling in his own name. In some circumstances, the word of neighbours or child's school cannot be relied upon because they may be protecting the individual from inquiries, or they may have been deceived into thinking that he has emigrated.

Passenger lists on all ships sailing from British ports, from 1890 to 1960, are in the Public Record Office in the Board of Trade papers, arranged by year and port of departure. Names, ages, occupations and usually former place of residence are included.

Records of removal firms and airlines may also reveal evidence of recent emigration (see pp. 147, 151).

Because payment of National Insurance is compulsory, the cessation of contributions as a result of emigration may be investigated by local offices of the DHSS; if they are satisfied by their researches that the individual has emigrated, the fact will be recorded by the Central Records branch at Newcastle; for accessibility, see pp. 98–9. If, however, child benefit is no longer claimed, the cause will not be investigated.

Women over sixty, men over sixty-five, and widows over fifty can arrange to have the pension, to which they are entitled as a result of paid-up contributions, paid to them abroad. Pension records of the DHSS may therefore be another source for learning of emigration. Currently, about 85,000 in Australia, 41,000 in Canada, 28,000 in the USA, 21,000 in New Zealand, 15,000 in South Africa and thousands of others in many countries round the world enjoy this facility (see the *Guardian*, 8 June 1985).

When anyone leaves a GP's patient list, whatever the cause, the NHS Central Register and FPC should be informed so that the GP's capitation income can be adjusted; (see pp. 50–8). Those still carrying their medical cards are invited to surrender them upon embarkation to Immigration Officials, who then forward them to the Central Register at Southport. However, this voluntary system is so far short of complete as a record of emigration that the OPCS does not use the resulting statistics as a basis for the IPS referred to above.

C40—Retirement pensions

Records of almost ten million pensioners in England, Wales and Scotland are maintained at the Longbenton site of the DHSS in Newcastle upon Tyne, and are computerised. The approach of retirement age triggers the National Insurance computer four months before the claimant reaches (at the time of writing) the age of sixty (women) or sixty-five (men). If no response is received to a letter sent to the last-known address inviting the claimant to confirm his personal data and make a claim for a state pension, no action is taken until the claimant 'surfaces' and ask for the pension to start. A second invitation is sent to women aged sixty-five and men aged seventy if a pension has still not been claimed by then.

Once a pension has been awarded, a number is allocated, using a somewhat archaic sequence invented in order to implement the 1936 Old Age Pensions Act which made pensions over the age of seventy non-contributory. The first four digits still record the week and year in which the claimant will reach the age of seventy, though, as this was based on a fifty-two-week year, there has been a progressive drift in the week number behind the true birthday. The next four characters in the pension number are issued sequentially; the fifth and eighth characters may be letters rather than digits. On the pension book there is also a serial number which changes for each claimant each time a new book is issued; it is related to the actual orders in that particular book.

The record at Newcastle includes the claimant's name, date of birth, present and former addresses (if addresses are frequently changed, the oldest will be progressively erased), information about marriage and the name/reference number of spouse, the rate of pension, and the payments issued. It records whether payment is by order book, payable order, or automatic credit transfer. In order book cases the record includes the post offices where payment has been arranged and changes of address or post office are kept up to date via the Post Office.

The system is indexed by name, by number, and by date of birth. The Registrar-General currently notifies Newcastle of the deaths of men born before 5 July 1883 and of women born before 5 July 1888, i.e. those too old to qualify for a death grant from the DHSS. (This grant amounts currently to less than ten per cent of the average cost of a funeral. A half-rate grant is available for women between the ages of fifty and sixty and for men between the ages of fifty-five and sixty-five at 5 July 1948.) In cases of hardship (some 13,000 in 1982), additional help may be available through the supplementary benefit scheme. The impact of the proposed abolition of the death grant on this flow of information is not yet clear, but would appear to make it redundant.

With the exception of a few pension records (such as some war pension payments which go back to the last century and are stored in local offices, not at Newcastle), most entries are erased from the computer two years after the pensioner's death, though a local office might keep a full record of the same individuals for five years. An abbreviated form of the notes, however, would be maintained on the National Insurance record indefinitely.

Access to the system is as described for National Insurance records; see pp. 97–9. Since the start of the 'contracting out' system in 1975, and 'carrying forward' pension schemes, considerable assistance is now given to insurance companies and former employers in tracing the present whereabouts of pensioners. Of particular use are contacts which can be made with pensioners who are living abroad because of the normal difficulty of discovering the fact of emigration by other means. See pp. 154–5.

C41—Death

Death creates more records than any other event in our lives. There is the doctor's certificate, possibly a hospital record, the bills of the undertaker and any other tradesman involved, the State registration of death, a grave register entry or an order for cremation; a burial or funeral service entry, the gravestone itself, with the monumental mason's copy, and will and associated documents, and if the death was in any way unusual, a coroner's report. It will not be unusual if my death generates over a dozen documents with several different institutions.

It is the State itself which registers death, using a system very similar to that by which births are recorded. It is very important to know how to discover whether someone has died in order to avoid wasting a lot of time and effort searching in the land of the living.

Unless the coroner is involved, a death must be registered within five days of the event or the discovery of the body, in the district where that took place. When the register books are completed, they are sent to the local superintendent registrar for permanent deposit. These books, dating from 1 July 1837, are not open to public inspection (apart from those which have not yet been completed) but anyone can buy a copy of any death entry. The superintendent registrar indexes those death entries, and the same conditions of public access to the indexes, and cost of certificates, apply as for birth indexes (see p. 48). The Registrar-General receives a copy of each entry, and once again makes indexes and copies available (see pp. 47–8).

Each death entry has the following data: the district and sub-district of registration; the entry number; the date and place of death; the name and surname; the sex of the deceased; occupation; usual address; name, surname, status, address, and signature of the informant; cause of death; date of registration; and signature of the registrar. Only since 1969 have the maiden surname in the case of a woman who has married and the date and place of birth (age before 1 April 1969) been entered.

The registrar sends copies of all death entries to the General Register

Office and thence to the relevant district medical officers; information about the deaths of particular individuals must also be sent to certain professional bodies if the deceased has been a practising or retired member thereof. These include dentists, doctors, druggists, midwives, opticians, pharmaceutical chemists, solicitors and veterinary surgeons. Similar documentation is forwarded concerning British Telecom, the Ministry of Defence, the Post Office, the DHSS, and some police and the Civil Service in respect of their pensioned staff. Copies of each draft death entry are sent to the NHS Central Register in Southport.

The national indexes of death for England and Wales are in St Catherine's House. Until 1969 these indexes provide the age at death; now they give the date of birth. This, however, is fallible, often being the 'best guess' of the informant (see Case Study A). The indexes are open to the public.

Some individuals will remain missing because although their deaths might be registered, their corpses have not been identified, and only the approximate age, sex, and circumstances of death will remain as a clue to the identity. The police, whose job it is to make the identification, should normally have a photograph, fingerprint, and dental record for circulation in the *Police Gazette*, to dentists, and so on. Help from dentists can be useful in confirming an identification, but otherwise, unless there is something very distinctive about the treatment which might trigger the dentist's memory, it would be an impossible task to go through all records. Specific requests are sometimes included in the *British Dental Journal*. Such details are not always available, and even when they are, the identity may remain a mystery. See, for example, *Police Review*, 9 September 1983. Of the fifty-two immediate victims of the Bradford City Football Club fire disaster on 11 May 1985, only twenty-eight could be identified by dental records. Up to half a dozen bodies a year are so mutilated that the sex is not determinable, and the registers also have to include ancient remains such as the men from the 'Mary Rose' or the two-thousand-year-old corpse discovered near Wilmslow, Cheshire, in 1984, though the latter has not been registered, it seems.

These are, however, only a small minority among the total unidentified, who number about fifty per annum. This figure has fallen dramatically since registration began in 1837, a graphic illustration of how our society has become more caring, more bureaucratic, or both. The annual totals were between 500 and 700 until the First World

War, fell to about 300 by the second, and to below 100 only in the 1950s with the advent of the NHS and National Insurance systems. Unidentified males are always several times more numerous than females.

Doctors, the police, or registrars of death refer to a coroner all cases in which death has occurred when no doctor had seen the deceased since death, or had not done so within fourteen days before death; when death had occurred during an operation or before the patient had recovered from the anaesthetic; when death was sudden, unexplained, or in suspicious circumstances; or when death might have been due to a number of causes, such as industrial injury, or offences against the person. If the coroner establishes that death is not due to natural causes, he will hold an inquest to establish the cause (not to prove the guilt of any party). In certain circumstances, the inquest must be with a jury, and the coroner has the power to call witnesses and evidence (including hospital case notes, for example).

Inquests are held in public unless the case involves national security. Any person having a 'proper interest' can see, or buy a copy of, the case notes less than seventy-five years old when they become known to the public. Those deemed to have such an interest are:

a parent, spouse, child and any person representative of the deceased;

any beneficiary of a policy for insurance on the life of the deceased, and any insurer having issued such a policy;

any person whose act or omission on the part of himself, his servants or agents, irrespective of whether it may give rise to civil liability, may, in the opinion of the coroner, have caused or contributed to the death of the deceased;

the chief officer of police (who may only examine witnesses through a lawyer);

any person appointed by a government department to attend the inquest;

any other person appealing to the coroner to have a proper interest.

The breadth of this access, and the fact that the inquest is in public, raises the question why access is not open to all.

Coroners retain their records for a maximum of only fifteen years, by which time they should be transferred to a public repository approved by the Lord Chancellor; (Coroners Rules 1984 and Home Office Circulars 250/1967 & 27/1971). At that time, most of the case papers are to be destroyed, and only certain ones selected for permanent preservation. These are indexed registers of deaths reported;

papers relating to treasure trove; matters resulting in substantive recommendations by the coroner; and extraordinary events, particularly those of historical, or wide public interest. It is the coroner, not the repository, who makes the selection for this permanent preservation.

I am pleased to say, however, that not all coroners carry out this act of destruction, especially as the documents are securely preserved in respositories and are therefore not demanding the coroner's own office space.

Having recorded a death, the registar will issue a green disposal certificate if the disposal is to be in England or Wales, retaining one part himself, a second part going to the place of disposal, and a third which is returned to the registrar afterwards. The recombination of the first and third parts is the only way that a death entry can be automatically connected to a place of disposal, but the registrars have to retain them for a minimum of only five years. Thus if you are researching a disposal over five years old, you might be dependent on a family memory or document to locate it; if, however, the informant on the death entry was from a social services department, or a firm of solicitors, they will probably be able to tell you which undertaker was used.

The National Association of Funeral Directors issues a directory of members, who operate to a code of ethics which reflects the very sensitive nature of the work they do. Some record of each client, usually quite a full record, is kept for as long as the firm lasts; those of a family firm may therefore extend back to the last century. The data recorded is normally: full name, title, age, date and place of death, home address, occupation, place of disposal (with a grave number if buried) of the deceased; the name and address of the person making the arrangements; the name of a minister and church involved; and any obituary notice placed in a local paper. (Some funeral directors place such a notice, especially in small towns, unless privacy has been requested; a list of all those attending the funeral may be included, but not all keep that record thereafter.)

Normally these records are maintained on a manual system, accessed by date and by name of deceased. The releasing of data is entirely at the discretion of the individual funeral director, and I have always found them sympathetic to a genuine enquiry.

There will probably be no other record of a funeral service. Churches and chapels will record the burial (or scattering of ashes) in their own graveyards, each denomination having its own form. Anglicans, for example, record name, age, address and date of burial on a form unaltered since 1813. The public has no right to inspect the burial register of any other denomination, but may have to pay for the privilege of seeing these in an Anglican church at the rate of £3.50 for the first hour (or part thereof) and £2.50 for each subsequent hour.

However, if burial occurred in a local authority cemetery (run by the 'Parks and Cemeteries' or even 'Recreation' Department), the office will maintain a much fuller record which will be open and normally free of charge to enquirers. You will probably find the names of the deceased, occupation, dates of death and burial, cause of death, age, and the place and number of the grave. The grave register contains the list of all persons interred in each, with dates and grave owner; a map will show the place of the grave in the cemetery; and finally any gravestone inscription might provide additional data concerning family relationships.

Most people who die nowadays are cremated. The majority of crematoria are maintained by local authorities, and the national Cremation Regulations lay down a greater amount of detail than that which is recorded in a burial register – name, residence, occupation, date of death and cremation, marital status, of the deceased; names and addresses of the persons applying for the cremation and signing the appropriate certificates, their relationship to the deceased, the district where the death was registered, and how the ashes were disposed of. (There appear to be no regulations limiting the ways in which ashes may be disposed of, short of causing public offence.) If a small plaque has been erected, it is unlikely to provide any information which is not on the register.

Since 1858, grants of representation relating to the estates of deceased persons have been the prerogative of the State. The Lord Chancellor's Department acts through the Principal Probate Registry (PPR) and a series of District Probate Registries (DPRs) issuing grants to executors of a valid will or to administrators (where there is no valid will, or no executors). The State has no responsibility for the actual distribution or administration of the estate.

Grants have been issued for only a minority of deceased persons. If they had had owned property registered in their name, such as a house, car or bank account, the grant is accepted by the registering authority as a prerequisite for transfer to the new owner, though banks can release without probate if the balance in the account is under £5,000.

Annual indexes to all grants in England and Wales are compiled, and those for the last fifty years (approximately) are open to public inspection in each DPR and in Somerset House. Once proved, wills themselves may be seen, and/or photocopies purchased, at either Somerset House (which holds copies of all wills proved in this country since 1858) or at the PPR or DPR where the will was proved. This public access applies only after the wills are proved; during the process itself, the documents come under Section 2 of the Official Secrets Act (1911), and in 1932 there was a successful prosecution of a Somerset House official for releasing information still *sub judice* to a reporter.

The indexes are often the most convenient way to discover the fact and date of a person's death (e.g. Case Study A), especially in the provinces, where the national death indexes are not available. The probate indexes are more properly called calendars, for they contain against each name additional data: the address, place of death, date and place of probate, the value of the estate and, until recently, the names of the executors. If no will was proved, any person to whom Letters of Administration were granted will also be found in the same calendars.

If there is something questionable about a will, the witnesses may be called to give evidence. There is no requirement that the addresses of witnesses be included on a will, and even if they are, it might have been signed so long ago that they have moved. In such cases, the onus to locate the witnesses lies with the applicant, not with the court, and any advice given by its officials will probably be to contact the deceased's neighbours, and to consult easily accessible sources such as the telephone book or the electoral register. If reasonable efforts have been made, unsuccessfully, to find the witnesses, the case will be referred to the Probate Registrar for his directions.

Intestacy may give rise to even more serious 'missing persons' problems, because there is a real danger that living relatives, even a separated spouse, may be overlooked during the distribution of the estate. The law lays down a sequence of relations having a claim to such an estate, starting with the spouse. It is the responsibility of the Probate Registry to establish to whom Letters of Administration should be issued, and usually that person presents himself to the court anyway.

Establishing the whereabouts of a missing spouse can be

particularly difficult, especially when a change of name is involved. The applicant will have to satisfy the registrar that the spouse *is* missing, and will probably be asked to complete a questionnaire concerning details about, and efforts to locate, him or her. If these efforts have been unsuccessful, the registrar will have to judge how to proceed on the basis of the replies.

Once appointed, it is the administrator who has to establish who, of the potential beneficiaries, is alive. If the advice of court officials is sought at that stage, the administrator will probably be referred to his solicitor; he, in turn, will almost certainly hire a competent professional searching agency under sub-contract; see p. 41.

As we have already seen (p. 40), executors can have particular difficulties in locating beneficiaries of certain types of bequest. To anyone acting in this capacity, the advice of court officials will probably be, once again, to consult a solicitor. (It must be remembered that their job ends with the distribution of the grant.)

When applying for documents relating to these grants, it is advisable to ask for all the documents in the same file. They are regarded as open to public access with the main wills themselves, though a registrar can reserve the right to withhold any which he regards as particularly sensitive.

Appendix I—Runaway children, agencies, and the law

The law relating to minors who are missing from their normal domicile is neither straightforward nor internally consistent. The rights of minors, and the rights and duties of various authorities towards them are to be found piecemeal across a number of statutes and regulations, with the result that present practices are based on a balance of interpretations and priorities rather than on the rigid application of a single code. One consequence is that practice can vary from place to place, and new practices develop within existing legal parameters.

Running away from home is not in itself an offence. (In contrast, Title III of the United States' Juvenile Justice Act, 1974, commonly known as the Runaway Youth Act, defined such an offender as 'a person under 18 years of age who absents himself away from home of legal residence without the permission of parents or legal guardian'.) In the UK, there are several statutory and other bodies which may be responsible for the care and control of minors, and they have at their disposal a wide range of powers which can be invoked if it is believed that some of the circumstances in which a runaway is living are such that they should be changed or constrained. The age of the minor is very important in this process. As a general guide:

- At fourteen, a child becomes a 'young person' reaching the 'age of discretion' at which he is deemed to be responsible for his own actions.
- At sixteen, the young person ceases to be of compulsory school age; can marry (with consent of parents or guardians); can enter full-time work, with a National Insurance number; is entitled to supplementary benefit (though since May 1985, there are domiciliary restrictions on the length of time a board and lodging allowance can be claimed); girls can consent to having sex with males; and the Matrimonial Proceedings Act, 1973 (S.3) recognises sixteen as 'the time at which a person becomes capable of having an independent domicile'.
- At seventeen, a young person becomes an adult in criminal law. Normally, they can no longer be made the subject of a care order or place of safety order.
- At eighteen, they are no longer a minor, being able to marry without consent, to vote, and are no longer regarded as being in the care and control of their parents. They are no longer regarded automatically as 'vulnerable' if reported to the police.
- At nineteen, teenagers can no longer be kept in local authority care.
- At twenty-one, they may legally consent to homosexual acts in private (male or female).

(Proposals to change many of these rules have been published by the Howard League, *Unlawful Sex*, 1985.)

When a minor runs away *from home*, there are various courses of action open to parties and institutions who may be involved. (*More stringent rules apply in the case of those who are absconding from care.*)

The minors themselves

If runaways under sixteen are convinced that their best interests would be served by an arrangement other than being returned to the homes from which they had fled, they can ask for parental control to be replaced by that of foster parents, the voluntary care of a local authority, or by wardship. If the runaway is under fourteen, it is most unlikely that a court receiving an application for wardship would respect the child's wishes, being below the age of discretion.

These options remain open for sixteen and seventeen-year-olds also; but from sixteen, minors have a chance of maintaining an independent existence, and cannot be forcibly returned to the parental home unless it can be shown that they are in moral or physical danger.

Parents

Parents have a number of agencies (notably the police, private detectives and the media) to assist in locating missing children, though the police will regard only those under seventeen as vulnerable by virtue of their age alone. The social services will not act as a tracing agent, but will offer to act as a go-between once the young person has been found and has expressed a wish not to return home; various voluntary agencies will perform the same role. All such agencies then find themselves in a difficult situation when they know that a sixteen to seventeen-year-old is living independently, and is apparently in no moral or physical danger, but the agency is approached by the parents wanting help to facilitate the young person's return home.

Formerly, parents also had recourse to habeas corpus to return their children, but the courts nowadays prefer wardship proceedings.

Social Services

The local authority has a general responsibility for the welfare of minors in their area. If it feels that the runaway, usually if under seventeen, is not receiving proper care and control from the parents, it can bring care proceedings under S.2 of the 1980 Child Care Act. This effectively replaces parental rights with those of the authority. However, S.1 of the same Act requires the authority to reduce the need to place children in care by facilitating a return to parent, guardian, relative, or friend. A common and useful device, therefore, is to apply for a magistrate's place of safety order, which lasts twenty-eight days, and gives the Department a breathing space to assess the situation (S.28 of the Children and Young Persons Act, 1969).

The police

The work of the police is basically to ensure that no harm befalls persons reported missing. 'Harm' may be the result of not only suicide or offences against the person, but also moral and physical injury resulting from the runaways' new environment. They may also detain youngsters who are apparently beyond the care and control of their parents. Much of this work is based on S. 28 of the Children and Young Persons Act, 1969. Section 28(2) reads:

> Any constable may detain a child or young person as respects whom the constable has reasonable cause to believe that any of the conditions set out in section 1(2) (a) to (d) of this Act is satisfied or that an appropriate court would find the condition set out in section 1(2) (b) of this Act satisfied or that an offence is being committed under section 10(1) of the Act of 1933 (which penalises a vagrant who takes a juvenile from place to place).

Sections 1(2) (a) to (d) read:

> If the court before which a child or young person is brought under this section is of the opinion that any of the following conditions is satisfied with respect to him that is to say – (a) his proper development is being avoidably prevented or neglected or his health is being avoidably impaired or neglected or he is being ill-treated; or
> (b) it is probable that the condition set out in the preceding paragraph will be satisfied in his case, having regard to the fact that the court or another court has found that that condition is or was satisfied in the case of another child or young person who is or was a member of the household to which he belongs; or
> (c) he is exposed to moral danger; or
> (d) he is beyond the control of his parent or guardian; . . . and also that he is in need of care or control which he is unlikely to receive unless the court makes an order under this section in respect of him, then, subject to the following provisions of this section and sections 2 and 3 of this Act, the court may if it thinks fit, make such an order.

The police may also have recourse to a number of other statutes which enable them to fulfil their obligations – for example, Sections 3 and 4 of the Vagrancy Act, 1824; Section 64 of the Metropolitan Police Act, 1839; Section 9 of the Law Reform (Miscellaneous Provisions) Act, 1949; and Part IV of the Police and Criminal Evidence Act, 1984.

Assisting runaways
There is an important difference between helping youngsters to run away in the first place, and helping once they have already left home. The former may be an offence under Section 56 of the Offences against the Person Act, 1861; Section 20 of the Sexual Offences Act, 1956 (in respect of girls under sixteen); or Section 2 of the Child Abduction Act, 1984 (in respect of under-sixteens). The actual charge would depend on the alleged motives of the accused.

Once a minor has run away from home, no-one is obliged to return them to their parents, the police, or any other authority, or even to reveal their whereabouts (unless that involves obstructing the police with their enquiries). This freedom to assist runaways does not apply in respect of those who have absconded from care – Sections 13–16 of the Child Care Act, 1980, make it an offence to assist or harbour those in such a category.

It has long been felt in some quarters that the operation of the laws indicated above deals unsatisfactorily with one group of youngsters in particular – those who are running away *from* a situation which has become intolerable to them. For the 'joyriders', those casually missing because they have omitted to indicate that they are staying with friends, or the absconders who return home, or go the friends, for Christmas, or at the time of some domestic crisis, for example, the law works efficiently enough; but for those who are escaping from a crisis, the normal force of the law is to return the runaway to the same situation – hence they run away again and again, becoming increasingly suspicious of the agencies which should be there to help them, and becoming more likely to be taken into care.

To try to ease this problem in Westminster and Camden in central London, the Children's Society has started the Central London Teenage Project. Their 'safe house' caters for up to ten youngsters who are either runaways from home and under seventeen, or absconders from care to the age of nineteen, and has the backing of the local authorities, the DHSS, and the police as a desirable experiment within the present law. The support of these agencies, which refer cases to the Project, *in effect* makes the accommodation a 'place of safety' without the need to go through a formal court procedure each time.

The object of the experiment is to provide thinking time not only for the youngsters but also for the Project workers, who assess the needs of the young, under-age runaways, provide a counselling service, and work out for each the best solution, in conjunction with parents or guardians and local authorities.

The runaways are returned to their home area or an alternative placement is found as quickly and effectively as possible. In each case all relevant police and social services departments are alerted to the fact that the youngster is safe and should no longer be considered missing. Meetings can be arranged between parents and the runaways, but the location of the 'safe house' is confidential to the Project and the supporting authorities. This helps to indicate to the youngsters that the Project has their welfare as its first priority.

In principle, there seems no reason why this scheme, if it proves successful, should not be extended to other major cities, given the goodwill of the authorities concerned. It may well be, however, that the needs of inner London, in terms of the numbers of runaways homeless in the city, are far greater than anywhere else in the country.

Another project was commenced by the National Children's Home (NCH) in December 1985. This will attempt to collate information on individual missing children nation-wide. The aims of the project will be modified by the outcome of research and by the results of the NCH's appeal for funding, but it is hoped that the police, local authorities, and parents will be helped, via a computerised directory, to find missing children. (Donations can be made through any branch of the Midland Bank or to the NCH 'Missing Link', Freepost, London N5 1BR.)

This work would continue the NCH's long tradition of assisting homeless children in London. An important innovation of the scheme would be research into running away from home in this country, in order to develop a taxonomy of causation.

Appendix II—Greater Manchester Police 'E' Division missing persons reports, 1984

'E' Division covers an area up to two miles wide and seven miles long, in the south of the city of Manchester, including most of Moss Side, Whalley Range, Rusholme, Fallowfield, Withington, Northern Moor, Baguley and Wythenshawe. The population is almost 120,000; but although this is several times less than the population of Norfolk, Suffolk, Dyfed-Powys, Gwent or North Wales, the Division receives more missing persons reports than each.

The recording system
The unit dealing with missing persons maintains three manual files:
(a) A series of chronologically consecutive books in which reports are entered as they are received. This provides the name of each person, the address from which they are missing, their age or date of birth, a rough indication of race, whether missing before, if known, how they were finally located, the type of institution from which they were missing, and the date of the report. During the latter half of 1984, the date of location was also entered. Complete data are not always available for each report; hence, in the analysis of 1,071 individual reports which follows, the total is not always the same.
(b) A file containing reports on each separate case, including the report forms filled in by the investigating officer.
(c) A cumulative card index of persons who have been the subject of reports, in alphabetical order, summarising the outcome of each report.

Interpretation
In the absence of any other similar analysis, it is important that the statistics from this Division should not be extrapolated, or even taken as typical, nationally. They are presented here to indicate the nature and extent of the problem of tracing missing persons in an inner-city area, and to indicate some of the complications behind the figures. It is all too easy to make assumptions about the causes of the patterns which follow, but there are usually several possible explanations for each, not necessarily mutually exclusive. For example, over half the reports concerned people missing from institutions, rather than from their own homes, and all the individuals who were reported missing more than four times in the year were from such institutions. This tells us little, however, about whether they were in any sense escaping, or running *towards* something outside; whether they were simply more *likely* to be reported missing because of the 'caring bureaucracy' and responsibilities of those institutions; or whether people with a tendency to wander are more likely to be found in institutions in the first place.

The only other area in England and Wales for which there exists any analysis corresponding to some of these headings is the Missing Persons

Bureau at New Scotland Yard, but as has already been noted (see p. 13), only a minority of persons reported missing from the Metropolitan area are included, and they are drawn from a much wider social environment. Nevertheless, where possible reference to figures kindly supplied by the Bureau has been made, for interest.

Section A – Main headings

1. Age
2. Sex
3. Race
4. Number of persons/Repeaters
5. Mode of return
6. Time away
7. Institutions
8. Month
9. Alone/accompanied
10. Distance travelled

Section B – Cross-tabulations

1.1 Age/sex
1.2 Age/race
1.3 Age/repeaters
1.4 Age/mode of return
1.5 Age/time away
1.6 Age/institution
1.7 Age/month

2.1 Sex/race
2.2 Sex/repeaters
2.3 Sex/mode of return
2.4 Sex/time away
2.5 Sex/institution
2.6 Sex/month

3.1 Race/repeaters
3.2 Race/mode of return
3.3 Race/time away
3.4 Race institution
3.5 Race/month

4.1 Repeaters/mode of return
4.2 Repeaters/time away
4.3 Repeaters/institution
4.4 Repeaters/month

5.1 Mode of return/time away
5.2 Mode of return/institution
5.3 Mode of return/month

6.1 Time away/institution
6.2 Time away/month

7.1 Insitutions/month

Key

Age = age of the individuals reported missing
Sex = sex of the individuals reported missing
Race = race of the individuals reported missing
Repeaters = whether individuals had been reported missing before, or are now for the first time
Mode of return = the circumstances leading to cancellation of the missing-persons report

Time away = interval between recording and cancellation
Institutions = place from which individuals were reported missing
MFH = missing from home, as opposed to an institution
Month = month of the year when reported missing

Section A

Age

Apart from a peak of 21 9-year-olds, reports concerning children at ages under 11 were in single figures. From 25 at age 11, figures double at each age, until 243 15-year-olds were reported. Those under fourteen formed 22 per cent of the total (twice the percentage of the same age group in London), thirteen to sixteens 60 per cent, and all those under seventeen, 71 per cent, (74 per cent in 1985). From the age of fifteen, however, the number of reports fell rapidly, with 102 16-year-olds, 34 aged 17, and only 8 aged 18. Apart from small peaks at age nineteen (11), 22 (15) and thirty-one (12), only a few were recorded at each adult age, until sixty-five to seventy-one when none was recorded. There was then a rise from seventy-two to eighty-six inclusive, the oldest missing during the year. Those in this age group formed 8 per cent of all reports, whereas those over sixty- five formed only 4 per cent in London. The average age of all missing persons in 'E' Division was twenty- two.

2 – Sex

Two-fifths of all reports concerned males (422), and the remainder females (649), a pattern repeated here in 1985. The figures for London in 1984 were forty-seven per cent and fifty-three per cent respectively.

3 – Race

Just over 80 per cent of the reports concerned white persons, 10 per cent black, and 10 per cent other races. Figures for London (on the Missing Persons Bureau's seven-point classification) for the first half of 1985 were: North European 1,686, Mediterranean 4, Negroid 477, Indian 152, Chinese 14, Arab 6, doubtful 90, and 157 being a combination of these categories.

4 – Repeaters

The 1,071 reports were generated by only 591 persons, 433 of whom were reported missing only once during the year, 76 twice, 26 three times, 19 four times, 8 five times, 6 six times, 5 seven times, 6 eight times, 3 nine times, 7 ten times, 2 eleven times, 1 twelve times, one 15-year-old girl seventeen times and one 78-year-old man twenty-two times. Six hundred and twenty-two reports concerned persons who had been reported missing before (not necessarily in 1984), whereas 402 were missing for the first time.

5 – Mode of return

Eight hundred and eighty-five returned of their own accord; 119 were traced by the police; a further thirty-three were detained (having absconded) and twenty-five arrested. Five were found dead. Only one was not found, but the report was cancelled as she was over seventeen years of age, and known to be alive and well subsequent to the report being filed.

6 – Time away

(Figures available for the second half of the year only.) Over 60 per cent were located within forty-eight hours, 87 per cent within a week, and 99 per cent within 3½ weeks. In London, 87 per cent were located after three months, and 99 per cent in over a year. The average time away (535 cases) was four days. There is no person registered as still missing from this Division from any period before 31 December 1984.

7 – Institutions

Forty-eight per cent of all reports received concerned persons missing from home (MFH); that is, missing from a private address. A further 29 per cent were missing from juvenile care, 8 per cent from hospitals (mostly from psychiatric wards), and the remainder from old people's homes.

8 – Month

Figures for each month were:

Jan	51 (425)	May	101 (494)	Sep	100 (463)
Feb	60 (379)	Jun	98 (431)	Oct	85 (471)
Mar	71 (445)	Jul	132 (500)	Nov	100 (419)
Apr	75 (421)	Aug	102 (478)	Dec	96 (361)

(Figures in brackets are for London, July 1984 to June 1985 inclusive.)

9 – Alone/accompanied

Some analysis was undertaken to examine the most common age groups for each sex to be reported missing. Of the 201 girls, 70 were from a juvenile institution. Of these, half disappeared singly, the other half went accompanied by at least one other. Of the other 30 per cent, all MFH, 28 per cent were missing on their own, and only 2 per cent had gone with at least one other person. The figures for fourteen- and fifteen-year-old boys showed exactly the same proportions, though the numbers were much lower.

10 – Distance travelled

Most of those missing returned of their own accord, so it is not possible to give an accurate indication of where they had been. From the cumulative card index, however, it was possible to identify those who had been traced, detained, arrested, or found dead, and get a rough idea of how far they had travelled in 158 cases. Of these, 114 were found within the city of Manchester (seven of whom had been taken to hospital), and a further fifteen (two in hospital) within a few miles of the city boundary. Ten were in adjoining counties in the North West, and 13 were scattered across other parts of the country. Of these, 6 went to London (5 persons, as one went twice) – 2 male adults, and 3 female absconders, aged fourteen (twice) and thirteen.

Section B

1.1 – Age/sex

Reports concerning boys under fourteen were more common than those for girls (148:85). This balance was reversed in the fourteen- to seventeen-year-olds (138 boys, 425 girls). Among adults, the sexes were evenly balanced (136 men, 138 women) but individual ages were distorted by a single individual being reported missing several times. The peak age for girls was fifteen, for boys fourteen (201:65). (The National Centre for Missing and Exploited Children in Washington reports that fifteen-year-old girls, who had been 'physically or sexually' abused at home is the most common category in the USA's much greater problem of missing persons.)

1.2 – Age/race

For most age groups up to eleven, the number of whites reported missing was roughly equal to all other races. Among the twelve to seventeen-year-olds, however, there was a large increase in the proportion of whites (575:126). The balance then returned among the eighteen to twenty-six-year-olds. Subsequently the proportion of whites increased with age – among the ages twenty-seven to eighty-six, 179:20. The peak at age twenty-two was largely among whites. Blacks formed about half the non-white individuals at all ages.

1.3 – Age/repeaters

The youngest person reported missing, but not for the first time, was aged five; but that only becomes a fairly common category from age eleven. There was a rise and fall in their numbers similar to the total figures, with a peak at fifteen. There were relatively few repeaters among ages 23–65, but then an increase in the seventy- and eighty-year-olds. Again, figures for individual ages can be distorted by one or two individuals who were reported missing several times during the year.

Those reported missing for the first time presented a different pattern. Most under the age of eleven were first-timers (53:26) but they formed a minority among the twelve- to seventeen-year-olds (217:458).

1.4 – Age/mode of return

Eight hundred and eight-five returned of their own accord, and their age pattern was similar to the overall age structure. About one in six were traced by the police, but among those (119 in all), the age pattern was far more distinctive, being more evenly spread than in direct proportion to the number reported missing. Of the 707 twelve to seventeen year-olds, 605 returned of their own accord, fifty were traced, a further twenty-eight detained, and

twenty-one arrested. These last two categories formed a significant proportion of all those found by the police above the age of ten, totalling thirty-four
and twenty-four respectively out of 183. Of those over seventy, sixty-six
returned on their own, and fifteen were traced. The five found dead were aged
twenty-eight, forty-six, forty-nine, fifty-six and seventy-three.

Thirteen missing spouses were traced during the year, and none returned
home as a result of being found. Nine were married (including 7 wives); the
others were 3 'common law' wives and one husband.

1.5 – Age/time away

Of the 535 reports for which the time spent away is available, only one
under the age of ten was missing for more than four days (a 9-year old, missing
for twelve days). The majority of most age groups were missing for less than
forty-eight hours. The longest away were three 16-year-olds (fifty-two,
seventy and eighty-six days), and one 14-year-old (eighty-one days). The only
age group missing in any significant numbers for more than seven days was
that of age thirteen to fifteen, only a third of which were away less than
forty-eight hours.

1.6 – Age/institutions

Although almost half of all reports concerned MFHs, they do not have the
same proportion in all age groups. They are under-represented among the
twelve to seventeens (303 out of 693) and among those over seventy (twenty-
two out of eighty), among whom the clear majority are missing from institutions.

1.7 – Age/month

All age groups, including those under ten and over seventy, show the same
overall pattern, avoiding January and February, and showing a peak in the
summer, especially July. There is a small peak of juvenile absconders at
Christmas time.

2.1 – Sex/race

There was roughly the same proportion of males to females (2:3) among all
races identified.

2.2 – Sex/repeaters

Of those reported missing in 1984, 43 per cent of the males and 36 per cent
of the females were missing for the first time.

2.3 – Sex/mode of return

The same percentage (just over eighty) of males and females returned of
their own accord. Of the remainder, females were over twice as likely to be
detained or arrested. Three males and 2 females were found dead.

2.4 – Sex/time away

Seventy per cent of males but only 52 per cent of females returned or were located within forty-eight hours. Only eight males remained away for more than a fortnight, whereas twenty-seven females did so. In London, individuals returned more slowly, but at first females returned more quickly than males (32:40 per cent within the same month). After three months, however, 85 per cent of both sexes had returned.

2.5 – Sex/institutions

There were rather more female than male MFHs (270:243), but the proportions were reversed among those missing from hospitals and old people's homes. The greatest discrepancy was among numbers of teenagers missing from juvenile care centres, girls far outnumbering boys (328:97). This was due in no small measure to the existence of a girls' assessment centre in the Division.

2.6 – Sex/month

Males and females were reported missing in roughly the same proportions in all months of 1984, though females had a slightly greater share in April, May, June and October, and girls were more likely than boys to abscond at Christmas. The MPB figures for 1984/5 show females marginally increasing their share from April to September.

3.1 – Race/repeaters

Thirty-seven per cent of whites, 44 per cent of blacks, and 49 per cent of other races were being reported missing for the first time.

3.2 – Race/mode of return

Over 90 per cent of blacks, and 82 per cent of whites and of other races, returned home of their own accord. The police traced some 12 per cent of whites, 8 per cent of blacks and 17 per cent of other races. Most of those detained (twenty-six) or arrested (twenty) from a total of fifty-eight were white, and all found dead were white. Five-sixths of over two hundred unidentified bodies reported to the MPB (January to July 1985) were 'Northern European'.

3.3 Race/time away

Only three non-whites (out of 108 known) stayed away for more than fifteen days, whereas twenty-seven out of 428 whites did so. Over 60 per cent of all races returned within forty-eight hours.

3.4 – Race/institutions

A little over 40 per cent of whites (but 60 per cent of blacks and of other races) were MFH. Forty per cent of whites (but only thirty per cent of all other races) were from juvenile centres, nine per cent of whites, but only 3 persons from other races, were from hospitals; the remainder were from old people's homes.

3.5 – Race/month

All races show the same pattern of report for each month, except for an 'other races' peak in December.

4.1 – Repeaters/mode of return

Just over 80 per cent of all missing persons returned home of their own accord whether they had been reported missing before or not. The police had more success at tracing those who were missing for the first time (15 per cent as opposed to 9 per cent). In contrast, four-fifths of those detained, and of those arrested, had been missing before. Four out of the five found dead had not been missing before.

4.2 – Repeaters/time away

About 60 per cent returned within forty-eight hours whether they had been reported missing before or not. About 6 per cent in each category stayed away for more than a fortnight.

4.3 – Repeaters/institutions

Most of the MFHs (293 out of 493) had not been missing before; in contrast, reports from all kinds of institutions, particularly the assessment centre (233 out of 285) and psychiatric wards (53 out of 58) show a majority with 'previous experience'. All those reported missing more than 4 times in the year (and two-thirds of those reported 4 times) were from institutions.

4.4 – Repeaters/month

Both categories followed a similar pattern, with fewer reports in the winter and more in the summer, especially July. Those missing for the first time, however, formed a higher than usual percentage in February and March.

5.1 – Mode of return/time away

Two-thirds of those who returned voluntarily did so within forty-eight hours. Forty-six per cent of those whom the police traced were found in the same period, as were about a third of those detained and of those arrested. Only 3 per cent of those returning voluntarily did so more than a fortnight after the report, whereas 20 per cent of those traced, detained or arrested had been away for the same period.

5.2 – Mode of return /institutions

Almost 80 per cent of MFHs returned home of their own accord; 13 per cent were traced by the police, and about 4 per cent detained or arrested. All 5 found dead were MFH. Those absconding from juvenile institutions were even more likely to return voluntarily (85 per cent); only 6 per cent of these were traced, leaving 9 per cent detained or arrested. (Girls formed five-sixths of this 6 per cent). Over 80 per cent of those missing from old people's homes and hospitals returned of their own accord.

5.3 – Mode of return/month

The figure of 80 per cent returning of their own accord applied to almost all months of the year, though it was rather less in July and August when over half the year's arrests occurred.

6.1 – Time away/institutions

Almost 60 per cent of MFHs returned within forty-eight hours; 54 per cent of juveniles from institutions and 90 per cent of those from hospitals and old people's homes did so. The only groups staying away for over a fortnight were 10 per cent of MFHs and 8 per cent of girls from the assessment centre.

6.2 – Time away/month

(Figures available for July to December only.) The month made little difference to the period of time spent away – about 60 per cent returned within forty-eight hours, and about half a dozen stayed away for more than a fortnight, in each month.

7.1 – Institutions/month

The MFHs were the most consistent in numbers across the year, the summer increase being only 66 per cent of the January figure. The pattern in old people's homes is similar. In contrast, there was a fivefold increase (January to July) in juveniles absconding from care, and in those from hospitals.

Case study B—The anonymous housewife

(Based on a programme first broadcast on BBC Radio 4 on 1 July 1983.)

A few years ago I bought a small, handwritten diary from a second-hand book stall. It had been written in 1932 by a housewife evidently living in the area of Gatley or Cheadle, to the south of Manchester, where she did her shopping. Neither her name nor her address is given, but there is a series of clues which at first sight might help to discover her identity.

1–On 8 January she received a birthday present.
2–Her husband, normally referred to as 'D.', was called Daniel.
3–She bought Daniel a birthday gift on 6 June.
4–On 21 April she bought him a present for their fifth wedding anniversary.
5–On 8 August their son Michael had his fourth birthday.
6–The diarist's mother-in-law lived at a house called 'Lyngarth' which was on, or near, Burton Road, West Didsbury, in south Manchester (i.e. this was the nearest bus stop).
7–The diarist lived next door to a Mrs Smith (whose daughter could one day be heard coughing, through the adjoining wall).
8–The bus stop nearest to their own home was on Cambridge Road in Gatley.
9–The family was on the telephone, Gatley receiving its first automatic system during the year.
10–On 18 May, her vacuum cleaner had to be repaired at 'Baxendale's'.
11–On 27 March, she 'carried Brenda up' to be christened in Irlam parish church.

Using information from the various sources in this book, can you work out (a) how to find out the age of the diarist in 1932; and (b) how I could have located her daughter, not yet born in 1932, who now lives in Scotland?

Select bibliography

AMMA (1985) Assistant Masters and Mistresses Association, *Report*, March 1985

Acheson, E. D., *Medical record linkage*, OUP, 1967.

Ackroyd, J. E., *The investigator: a practical guide to private detection*, Frederick Muller, 1974

Aitken, J. *Officially secret*, Weidenfeld & Nicholson, 1971

Akehurst, M., *Running to the city*, National Association of Youth clubs, n.d.

Anderson, I. G., *Current British directories*, CBD Research Ltd., 9th ed., 1979

Angus, J. *et al.*, *The Tayside Master Patient Index*, Tayside Health Board, 1978

Benjamin, B. (ed.), *Medical records*, William Heinemann Medical Books Ltd., 2nd ed., 1980

Bevan, H. K. & Parry, M. L., *Children Act 1975*, Butterworth, 1979

Bok, S., *Secrets: on the ethics of concealment and revelation*, OUP, 1984

Booth, N. D., *Social Security contributions*, Butterworth, 1962

Bourn, C. & Benyon, J., *Data protection*, University of Leicester Continuing Education Unit, 1983

Brandon, D. *et al.*, *The survivors*, Routledge & Kegan Paul, 1980

Brennan, T. *et al.*, *The social psychology of runaways*, Lexington Books, 1978

British Journal of Preventive and Social Medicine

Buckland, Y., (ed.), *Approaches to problems in records management No 1 – Personnel Records*, Records Management Group of the Society of Archivists, 1985

Bulmer, M. (ed.), *Censuses, surveys and privacy*, Macmillan, 1979

Card, R., *Estate Agents Act, 1979*, Butterworth, 1979

Children's Legal Centre, *Working with young children*, December 1983
Running away, information sheet, 1985

Commission for Racial Equality, *Code of practice: race relations*, CRE, 1983

Collin, W. G., *Introducing computer programming*, National Computing Centre, 1974

Coote, A. & Grant, L., *Civil liberty: the NCCL guide*, Penguin, 1973

County Court Practice – *see* Gregory, R. C. L.

Cox, B., *Civil liberties in Britain*, Penguin, 1975

Cracknell, R., *Clues to the unknown*, Hamlyn, 1981

Davies, M. R. R., *The law of burial, cremation and exhumation*, Shaw & Sons, 4th ed., 1976

Delbridge, R. & Smith, M. (eds.), *Consuming secrets: how official secrecy affects everyday life in Britain*, Barnet Books, 1982

Drury, M., *The medical secretary's handbook*, Baillière Tindall, 1975

Dyer, B., *Personnel systems and records*, Gower Press, 3rd ed., 1979

Eaton, J. & Gill, C., *The trade union directory*, Pluto Press, 1981
Efficiency Scrutiny Report: *Registration of births, marriages and deaths*, February 1985
Ellison, M., *Missing from home*, Pan Books, 1964
English, J. & Houghton, R., *Police training manual*, McGraw Hill, 2nd ed., 1978
Flaherty, D. H., *Privacy and government data banks*, Mansell, 1979
Franks Report: Departmental Committee on Section 2 of the Official Secrets Act (1911), 4 vols., Cmnd. 5104, 1972
GMC, *Professional conduct and discipline: fitness to practise*, April 1985
Gregory, R. C. L., *The County Court Practice, 1984*
Hansard
Hewitt, P., *Privacy: the information gatherers*, NCCL, 1977
Jackson, J. (ed.), *Rayden's Law and practice in divorce and family matters*, Butterworth, 14th ed., 1983
Jarvis, F. V., *Probation officer's manual*, Butterworth, 3rd. ed., 1980
Jones, M. (ed.), *Privacy*, David & Charles, 1974
Jones, R. V. H. *et al.*, *Running a practice*, Croom Helm Ltd., 1981
Josling, J. F., *Change of name*, Oyez Longman, 1985
Justice, *Privacy and the law*, Stevens & Sons, 1970
Körner, E. (chm), *First reports of steering group on Health Services Information*, HMSO, 1982
A report from the confidentiality working group, unpublished, 1984
Law Commission, *Breach of confidence*, Working Paper No. 58, 1974
Lawton, R., *The census and social structure*, Cass, 1978
London & Birmingham, 1968: The London and Birmingham Registrars' Groups of the Corporation of Secretaries, *Share registration in practice*, Editype, 1968
Mackenzie, W. J. M., *Power and responsibility in health care*, OUP, 1979
Mackichan, N. D., *The GP and the Primary Health Care Team*, Pitman Medical, 1976
Madgwick, D. & Smythe, T., *The invasion of privacy*, Pitman, 1974
Masson, J., Norbury, D. & Chatterton, S. G., *Mine, yours or ours?*, HMSO, 1984
Mathews, A. S., *The darker reaches of government*, University of California Press, 1978
Mills, J., (Wurtzburg & Mills), *Building Society Law*, Stevens & Sons, 1976
Moriarty's Police Law, Butterworth, 1981 ed.
National Association for the Care and Resettlement of Offenders, *School reports in the Juvenile Court*, NACRO, 1984
National Consumer Council, *Consumers and credit*, NCC, 1980.
National Register, United Kingdom and Isle of Man: statistics of population, HMSO, 1944
NORCAP, *Searching for family connections*, unpublished, n.d.
Police Review

Population Trends
Pounder, C., *Police computers and the Metropolitan Police*, Greater London Council, 1985
Rayden on Divorce, *see* Jackson, J.
Report of the Committee on abuse of social security benefits, Cmnd. 5228, 1973
Robertson, K. G., *Public secrets: a study in the development of government secrets*, Macmillan, 1982
Robertson, R., 'Salvationism's centenary', *New Society*, vol. 144, 1 July 1965
Rogers, C. D., *The family tree detective*, Manchester University Press, 1985
Rowe, B. C. (ed.), *Privacy, computers and you*, National Computing Centre, 1972
Rule, J. B., *Private lives and public surveillance*, Allen Lane, 1973
Savage, N. & Edwards, C., *A guide to the Data Protection Act, 1984*, Financial Training Publications, 1984
Society of Archivists, Records Management Group, *The records of social services departments: their retention and management*, 1982
Street, H., *Freedom, the individual, and the law*, Penguin, 1967 ed.
Terry, J., *A guide to the Children Act, 1975*, Sweet & Maxwell, 1979
Todd, J. E. & Dodd, P. A., *The electoral registration process in the United Kingdom*, OPCS, 1982
Toynbee, P., *Lost children*, Hutchinson, 1985
Treanor. W. W. (ed.), *National directory of runaway programs*, National Youth Work Alliance, 4th ed., 1979
Triseliotis, J., *In search of origins*, R&KP, 1973
New developments in foster care and adoption, Routledge & Kegan Paul, 1980
Wiggans, A., *Away from the bright lights: youth work and homelessness*, GMYA/NAYC Homelessness Project, 1982
Williams, R., *Missing! A study of the world-wide missing persons enigma and Salvation Army response*, Hodder & Stoughton, 1969
Young, J. B. (ed.), *Privacy*, John Wiley, 1978
Younger Report: *Report of the Committee on Privacy*, Cmd. 5012, 1972

Some useful addresses

Association of British Investigators, ABI House, 10 Bonner Hill Road,
  Kingston-upon-Thames, Surrey KT1 3EP
Bonds and Stock Office, Lytham St Annes, Lancashire FY0 1YN
Business Lists UK, 27 Manor Road, Bramhall, Stockport SK7 3LX
CCN Systems Ltd, Talbot Street, Nottingham NG1 5HF
The Children's Legal Centre Ltd, 20 Compton Terrace, London N1 2UN
The Children's Society, London and South East Regional Office,
  363a Kennington Road, London SE11 4QD
Companies Registration Office, Companies House, Crown Way, Maindy,
  Cardiff CF4 3UZ
Department of Education and Science (Personnel Records), Mowden Hall,
  Staindrop Road, Darlington, Co. Durham DL3 9BG
Department of Health and Social Security Special Section 'A', Records
  Branch, Central Office, Longbenton, Newcastle upon
  Tyne NE98 1YX
Department of Transport, Driver and Vehicle Licensing Centre, Longview
  Road, Swansea SA6 7JL
General Register Office, St Catherine's House, 10 Kingsway,
  London WC2B 6JP
General Register Office, Titchfield, Fareham, Hants PO15 5RR
Inland Revenue Management Division (Personnel and Accommodation),
  Section M1/5C, NW Wing, Bush House, Aldwych,
  London WC2B 4PP
Institute of Professional Investigators, 31a Wellington Street, St John's,
  Blackburn BB1 8AF
'Link Up', Exchange and Mart, Link House, 25 West Street, Poole,
  Dorset BH15 1LL
Ministry of Defence – see pp. 83–5
Missing Persons Bureau, New Scotland Yard, Broadway,
  London SW1H 0BG
National Children's Home, 85 Highbury Park, London N5 1UD
National Council for Civil Liberties, 21 Tabard Street, London SE1
National Health Service Central Register, Smedley Hydro, Southport,
  Merseyside PR8 2HH
National Organisation for the Reunion of Child and Parent, 49 Russell Hill
  Road, Purley, Surrey CR2 2XB
National Youth Bureau, 17–23 Albion Street, Leicester LE1 6GD
Office of Population Censuses and Surveys, St Catherine's House,
  10 Kingsway, London WC2B 6JP
Passport Department, Clive House, 70–78 Petty France,

London SW1H 9HD

Principal Registry of the Family Division, Somerset House, Strand, London WC2R 1LP

Principal Probate Registry, Somerset House, Strand, London WC2R 1LP

The Reunion Register, 2 Milton Court Farm Cottages, Westcott, Dorking, Surrey RH4 3NA

Salvation Army Social Services Investigation Department, 110–112 Middlesex Street, London E1 7HZ

Title Research (Administration) Ltd, Africa House, 64–78 Kingsway, London WC2B 6AH

United Association for the Protection of Trade, Zodiac House, 163 London Road, Croydon CR9 2RP

United Kingdom Central Council for Nursing, Midwifery and Health Visiting, 23 Portland Place, London W1N 3AF

Index

Ace Detective Agency, 101
administration of estates, *see* probate
Adopted Children Register, 61–2, 65
adoption, 4, 9, 10, 31, 37, 43, 55, 57,
  59–68, 96, 112–13, 141
Adoption Act (1958), 61, 65, 68
affiliation, 57, 68–9
Air Force Act (1955), 86
'alpha' listing (electoral registers),
  107–9
Amalgamated Union of Engineering
  Workers, 90
Armed Forces Act (1966), 86
Army Act (1955), 86
army records, *see* Ministry of
  Defence
Association of British Investigators,
  35–6
Association of Chief Police Officers,
  13, 146
Association of Health Care
  Information and Medical Records
  Officers, 146
'attainers', 104, 107

Bankers' Books Evidence Act
  (1879), 77
banks, bank accounts, 17, 37, 73–81,
  83, 99, 115, 117–18, 123, 132, 134,
  147
bank trust companies, 39–43, 57, 82,
  91, 94, 131, 134
baptism, 58, 65
Barclays Bank, 74, 76
'Benjamin Order', 41
birth counsellors, 61, 66–7
birth, registration of, 9, 47–8, 53, 59,
  61–3, 65, 68
Bonds and Stock Office, 133–4
British Airways, 151

British Association of Removers, 147
British Broadcasting Corporation,
  42–3
British Caledonian, 151
British Medical Association, 88, 91,
  146
British Telecom, 127–31, 141, 158
Bruinvels, P., 2
building societies, 17, 24, 74, 79–80,
  99, 115–19, 123–6
burial records, 160–1
Business Lists UK, 78

CCN Systems, 37–8, 75
cemeteries, 161
census, 109–10
Central London Teenage Project,
  167
change of name, *see* name, change of
Chester, Charlie, 43
Chief Registrar of Friendly
  Societies, 119
Child Abduction Act (1984), 166
child benefit, 24, 64, 68, 96–7,
  114–15
Child Care Act (1980), 165, 167
child health programme, 112–13
Children Act (1975), 61, 64, 66, 68
Children and Young Persons Act
  (1969), 165–6
Children's Society, The, 167
Church of England records, 58–9,
  65, 103, 161
Citizens Advice Bureau, 25, 44, 106
Civil Aviation Authority, 141, 151
clairaudients, clairvoyants, 19–20
colleges, 72–3
Commission for Racial Equality, *see*
  Race Relations Board
'Community Index', *see* Master

Patient Index
Companies Acts (1948, 1967), 120
Companies Registration Office, 120–1
'contact tracing', 113
coroners, 157, 159–60
corpses, unidentified, 18, 158
cremation, 161
Criminal Records Office, 111, 139–40
Customs & Excise, 99, 101, 130, 136, 142, 146, 148, 151

Data Protection Act (1984), 1, 11, 39, 68, 71–2, 80, 100, 108, 141
Day of the Jackal, 149
death, 157–63
death grant, 97, 156
Declaration of Geneva (1947), 50
deeds poll, 9
dentists, dental records, 48–9, 141, 158
Department of Education and Science, 70, 91–2, 141
Department of Employment, 86–7, 95, 99
Department of Health and Social Security, *passim*
Department of Transport, 135–6
deserters, military, 86, 141
Diocesan Record Offices, 59
Diplomatic Privileges Act (1964), 151
Director-General of Fair Trading, 77, 121
directories, telephone, *see* phone books; trade and householders', 107, 125
Disqualified Drivers Index (PNC), 140
District Health Authorities, 51, 64–5, 112–13
District Medical Officers, 105, 112
District Probate Registries, 161–2
divorce records, 31, 37, 96, 153–4

doctors, 48–54, 56, 63, 85, 91, 111–13, 141, 143, 145, 155, 157–9
dowsers, 19
Driver and Vehicle Licensing Centre, 79, 135–8
drivers register, 135–6
driving licences, 5, 79, 135–6, 140
druggists, 158

electoral registers, 10, 38, 58, 67, 103–9, 162
electricity boards, 116, 127–8, 131
emigration, 96, 98, 113, 147–8, 154–5, 157
employers' records, 33, 76, 78–86, 95
estate agents, 121–3
Estate Agents Act (1979), 121
Exchange and Mart, 44–5
Exchequer & Audit, 99

family allowance, *see* child benefit
Family Practitioner Committees, 48–52, 54–8, 63, 144, 155
Foreign Office, 99
fostering, 59, 63–4, 141
Franks Committee, Report, 7, 51, 87, 101, 129
funeral directors, 157

gas boards, 127–8, 131
General Medical Council, 50
general practitioners, *see* doctors
General Register Office, 48, 51, 62, 65–8, 97, 100, 103–4, 106, 156, 158
grave registers, 157, 161
guardians *ad litem*, 60–1

hacking, 38
heath and safety authorities, 99
health visitors, 64, 93–4, 112–13
Hindus, 58
Hippocratic Oath, 50
holiday records, 150–1

Home Office, 24, 36, 51, 73, 77, 92, 98–9, 104, 106–7, 110, 131, 138–40, 142, 148–9, 154
hospitals, 18, 24, 48, 54, 64, 95–6, 143–7, 157
hotel records, 151–2
house deeds, 124
Huckfield, L., 2

identity, proof of, 47, 54, 152
illegitimacy, 31, 60, 68–9
immigration, 51, 65
impersonation, 39, 87, 105, 149
Incorporated Society of Valuers and Auctioneers, 121
Independent Broadcasting Authority, 42
Inland Revenue, 37, 74, 80, 95–6, 99–102, 106, 118, 125, 136, 142, 147
Inner London Education Authority, 71
Institute of Personnel Management, 81
Institute of Professional Investigators, 35–6
insurance records, 5, 83
Interception of Communications Act (1985), 131, 143
International Find-a-Child, 44
International Passenger Survey, 154
intestacy, 40, 162–3

Janner, G., 2, 29, 101
journalists, 4–5, 77, 82, 146
jury service, 104

Körner reports, 54, 113, 143–6

Land Registry, 125
Law Reform (Miscellaneous Provisions) Act (1949), 166
Law Society, The, 122
'leg work' defined, 10
'List 99', 92

Lloyds Bank, 76
local education authorities, 70–1, 92, 113
Lockwood case, 78
London Gazette Supplement, 134

McGregor, O. R., 33
Midland Bank, 74–6
maintenance, 57, 69
Manchester Evening News, 44–5
marriage, 66, 102–3
Master Patient Index, 52, 144
maternity grant, 114
Matrimonial Proceedings Act (1973), 164
media, the, 18, 40, 42–6
Medical Records Officers, 144–6
medical research, 56–8, 82, 97–8
Metropolitan Police Act (1839), 166
midwives, 48, 64, 93–4, 141, 158
Ministry of Defence, 5, 83–6, 99, 137, 152, 158
missing adults, 4, 12–20, 25–30
missing minors, 12, 20–5, 118–19, 164–77
missing persons, defined, 1, 12, 164; long-term, 27–30; radio appeals for, 42; statistics, 1, 12–30, 170–7; in USA, 2–3, 20, 25, 28, 44–6, 164, 173; and unemployment, 15; and urbanisation, 16–17
Missing Persons Bureau, 13–14, 16–18, 23, 27, 29
mortgages, 118, 123–5
Mothers' Union, 25
murders, 23, 27

name, change of, 8–9, 33, 62–4, 70, 80, 96, 98, 100, 149, 163
Names Indexes (PNC), 139–40
National Association of Estate Agents, 121
National Association of Funeral Directors, 160
National Association of Local

Government Officers, 89–90
National Children's Home, 167–8
National Health Service Central Register, 48, 50–8, 63, 109, 117, 155–6, 158
National Health Service number, 6, 24, 47–56, 63–5, 96, 137, 143–4
National Identity number, 53, 109
National Insurance, 5, 24, 54, 64, 79, 81, 87, 94–100, 114–15, 154–5, 164
National Organisation for the Reunion of Child and Parent, 67–8
National Television Licence Records Office, 131, 133
National Union of Mineworkers, 89
National Union of Public Employees, 90
National Westminster Bank, 74–6
National Women's Aid Federation, 10
Naval Discipline Act (1961), 86
News of the World, 40, 44
newspapers, 43–6
Notification of Births Act (1907), 112
numbering systems for individuals, 5–6, 53–4, 65, 73–4, 80, 91, 93, 95–6, 100, 112–14, 116, 124, 126–7, 132–3, 135–6, 140, 149, 155–6
nurses, 93–4, 141

Offences against the Person Act (1861), 166
Office of Fair Trading, 36, 77
Office of Population Censuses and Surveys, 50, 109, 154
Office of Telecommunications, 130
Official Secrets Act (1911), 2, 6–7, 57, 79, 83, 87, 98, 100–1, 110, 127, 129, 132–3, 135, 137, 141, 148, 153, 162
Old Age Pensions Act (1936), 155
opticians, 48–9, 158

Parochial Registers and Records Measure (1978), 58–9
passports, 148–50, 154
Paymaster-General, 92
payrolls, 79–81
pensions, 79, 96, 154–7
personnel records, *see* employers' records
phone books, 107, 129, 162
police, 12–30 *et passim*
Police and Criminal Evidence Act (1984), 146, 166
Police Gazette, 18, 158
Police National Computer, 18, 86, 137–42
poll-tax, 104, 106, 125
polytechnics, 72–3
Post Office, 54, 99, 116, 130, 134, 141–3, 156, 158
Post Office Users National Council, 130
premium bonds, 133–4
Principal Probate Registry, 161–2
prison records, 51, 94, 96, 110–11
private detectives, 35–9 *et passim*
Pratt, Lt. Col. B., 34
probate, 39–42, 157, 161–3
probation records, 110–11
professional associations, 88–91
Public Record Office, 9, 100, 149, 154

Quakers, 58

Race Relations Board, 90–1, 142
rates, 125–7
Registrar of Companies, 120
Registrar-General, *see* General Register Office
removal firms, 147–8, 154
rents, 125–7
retirement pensions, 5, 96–7, 154–7
Reunion Register, the, 44
Roman Catholic records, 58

Royal Air Force, *see* Ministry of Defence
Royal Institute of Chartered Surveyors, 121
Royal Mail redirection service, 142–3
Royal Navy, *see* Ministry of Defence
Russell Soundex code, 112

'safe houses', 25, 167
St Catherine's House *see* General Register Office
Salvation Army, 30–4 *et passim*
Samaritans, 130
school records, 58, 70–1
Sexual Offences Act (1956), 166
shareholders, records of, 38, 119–21, 125
social services departments, 4, 24, 31, 60–1, 67–8, 111
SOGAT '82, 88–9
Special Section 'A', 97, 115
Spotlight, 88
Stonehouse, J., 149
students, *see* school records
supplementary benefit, 95, 156, 164

Tate, G., 19, 44
Tate, J., 44
teachers, 79, 91–2
telephones, bugging of, 39; directories, *see* phone books; *see also* British Telecom
television, licences, 131–2; rental, 132–3
Thatcher, D., 77
Title Research, 41
trade unions, 73, 88–91
Trades Descriptions Act (1968), 142

Transport and General Workers Union, 89–90
travel agents' records, 150–1
Treasury Solicitor, 40
Trustee Savings Bank, 75–6, 78

undertakers, *see* funeral directors
unemployment, 15, 86–7
Union of Shop, Distributive and Allied Workers, 89
United Association for the Protection of Trade, 37–8, 75
United Kingdom Atomic Energy Authority, 141
United Kingdom Central Council for Nursing, Midwifery, and Health Visiting, 93–4
universities, 72–3

Vagrancy Act (1824), 166
Vehicle Excise Act (1971), 137
Vehicle Identification Number, 79, 137, 139
Vehicle Owners Index (PNC), 138–9
Vehicle Register, 136–8
veterinary surgeons, 158

Wanted and Missing Persons, Index of (PNC), 140
water boards, 127–8
Williams & Glyn's Bank, 76
wills, *see* probate

Young Men's Christian Association, 152
Younger Committee, Report, 36, 38, 77, 101